THE UNOFFICIAL RECIPE GUIDE

T0024663

The

"I LOVE MY INSTANT POT®"

VEGAN

Recipe Book

From *Banana Nut Bread Oatmeal* to *Creamy Thyme Polenta*,
175 Easy and Delicious Plant-Based Recipes

Britt Brandon, CFNS, CPT

Adams Media

New York   London   Toronto   Sydney   New Delhi

This book is dedicated to my kiddos, the three lights of my life:
Lilly, Lonni, and JD. You make every second in the kitchen a fun adventure
that fills my life with memories I will cherish for a lifetime!

Adams Media
An Imprint of Simon & Schuster, Inc.
57 Littlefield Street
Avon, Massachusetts 02322

First Adams Media trade paperback edition DECEMBER 2017

ADAMS MEDIA and colophon are trademarks of Simon and Schuster.

For information about special discounts for bulk purchases, please contact Simon & Schuster Special Sales at 1-866-506-1949 or business@simonandschuster.com.

The Simon & Schuster Speakers Bureau can bring authors to your live event. For more information or to book an event contact the Simon & Schuster Speakers Bureau at 1-866-248-3049 or visit our website at www.simonspeakers.com.

Interior design by Colleen Cunningham
Photographs by James Stefiuk

Manufactured in the United States of America

10 9 8 7 6 5 4 3

Library of Congress Cataloging-in-Publication Data
Brandon, Britt, author.
The "I love my Instant Pot®" vegan recipe book / Britt Brandon, CFNS, CPT.
Avon, Massachusetts: Adams Media, 2017.
Series: "I Love My".
Includes index.
LCCN 2017030567 (print) | LCCN 2017031940 (ebook) | ISBN 9781507205761 (pb) | ISBN 9781507205778 (ebook)
LCSH: Pressure cooking. | Vegan cooking. | BISAC: COOKING / Methods / Special Appliances. | COOKING / Vegetarian & Vegan. | COOKING / Courses & Dishes / General. | LCGFT: Cookbooks.
LCC TX840.P7 (ebook) | LCC TX840.P7 B73 2017 (print) | DDC 641.5/636--dc23
LC record available at https://lccn.loc.gov/2017030567

ISBN 978-1-5072-0576-1
ISBN 978-1-5072-0577-8 (ebook)

Contains material adapted from the following titles published by Adams Media, an Imprint of Simon & Schuster, Inc.: The Everything® Vegetarian Pressure Cooker Cookbook by Amy Snyder and Justin Snyder, copyright © 2010, ISBN 978-1-4405-0672-7; and The "I Love My Instant Pot®" Recipe Book by Michelle Fagone, copyright © 2017, ISBN 978-1-5072-0228-9.

Contents

Introduction

The Instant Pot®.

Today it seems like almost everyone has one, but you may not know what it can do, what to expect, or even what an Instant Pot® actually is. If that sounds familiar, don't worry. Throughout *The "I Love My Instant Pot®" Vegan Recipe Book*, you'll learn everything you need to know about this appliance and how and why you should use it.

Cooking with an Instant Pot® will change the way you think about cooking. Why? Because it is a multifunction cooking appliance. It is a pressure cooker, a rice cooker, a slow cooker, a sauté pan, and more all rolled into one. It can cook everything from soups to cheesecakes! And the high-pressure cooking and steaming ability of an Instant Pot® does wonders for vegetables, tofu, beans, and a multitude of other ingredients. These modern, cutting-edge workhorses are sleek, efficient, and easy to operate. The Instant Pot® allows you to prepare healthy meals in minutes rather than hours with just the touch of a button. This cooking method also seals in essential vitamins and minerals and allows you to turn out healthier, better-tasting food that is perfect when you're on the go.

If you're worried about safety, don't be. Today these appliances have various certified safety mechanisms depending on the model, including a lockable lid, pressure regulator, leaky lid smart detection, anti-blockage vent, magnetic sensor for lid position detection, automatic pressure control, automatic temperature control, and power fuse cutoff. These safety measures take the worry out of pressure cooking.

Whether you just brought home your first Instant Pot® or you have been using one for years, the more than 175 delicious dishes in this cookbook will show you just how versatile the Instant Pot® really is. You'll discover that you can make everything from hearty breakfasts like Spinach and Portobello Benedict to amazing main courses like Creole Jambalaya and Seitan Sloppy Joes to delicious desserts like Spiced Chocolate Cake.

In this book you'll find everything you need to know about how to use your Instant Pot®, including how to clean it, how to use the buttons, and what you should have on hand to make your Instant Pot® dishes even better. So plug in your Instant Pot® and get ready to enjoy some amazing, quick meals.

Cooking with an Instant Pot®

So you're about to venture into the amazing world of Instant Pot® cooking...but you're not sure where or how to start. Don't worry, this chapter will give you the information you need to know to get started. Here you'll learn what all those buttons on your Instant Pot® do, how to release the pressure from the Instant Pot® when the cooking time is up, how to keep your Instant Pot® clean, and more.

Even though you'll learn all this information in this chapter, it's important that you read the owner's manual as well. The user manual is your key to successfully creating the recipes throughout this book. In addition to pointing out the basic functions of the appliance, it will tell you to do an initial test run using water to get familiar with the Instant Pot®. I can't stress enough that you need to do this. It will familiarize you with this appliance and take away some of the anxiety. In addition, this first run will help steam-clean your pot before you use it to make a favorite recipe.

But for now, let's take a look at some Instant Pot® basics.

Function Buttons

You are staring at the Instant Pot® and there are so many buttons. Which one should you use? Most of the function buttons seem obvious, but it is important to note that several are set with preprogrammed default cooking times. Also, every button option on the Instant Pot® initiates 10 seconds after you hit the button. Mostly likely, you will utilize the Manual button the most because you are in complete control, but read on for more detailed information on the remaining function buttons.

Manual button. This might be your most used button on the Instant Pot®. The default pressure setting is High; however, you can toggle the pressure from High to Low by pressing the Pressure button. Use the Plus and Minus buttons to adjust the pressurized cooking time.

Sauté button. This button helps the Instant Pot® act as a skillet for sautéing vegetables or searing meat prior to adding the remaining ingredients of a recipe, and it is used for simmering sauces as well. There are three temperature settings—Normal, Less, and More—that can be accessed using the Adjust button. The Normal setting is for sautéing, the Less setting is for simmering, and the More setting is for searing meat. Keep the lid open when using the Sauté button to avoid pressure building up.

Soup button. This button is used to cook soups and broths at high pressure for a default of 30 minutes. The Adjust button allows you to change the cooking time to 20 or 40 minutes.

Porridge button. This button is used to cook porridge, congee, and jook in the Instant Pot® at high pressure for a default of 20 minutes. The Adjust button allows you to change the cooking time to 15 or 40 minutes.

Poultry button. This button is used to cook chicken, turkey, and even duck at high pressure for a default of 15 minutes. The Adjust button allows you to change the cooking time to 5 or 30 minutes.

Meat/Stew button. This button is used to cook red meats and stews at high pressure for a default of 35 minutes. The Adjust button allows you to change the cooking time to 20 or 45 minutes.

Bean/Chili button. This button is used to cook dried beans and chili at high pressure for a default of 30 minutes. The Adjust button allows you to change the cooking time to 25 or 40 minutes.

Rice button. This button is used to cook white rice such as jasmine or basmati at low pressure. The Instant Pot® automatically sets the default cooking time by sensing the amount of water and rice in the cooking vessel.

Multigrain button. This button is used to cook grains such as wild rice, quinoa, and barley at high pressure for a default of 40 minutes. The Adjust button allows

you to change the cooking time to 20 or 60 minutes.

Steam button. This button is excellent for steaming veggies and seafood using your steamer basket. It steams for a default of 10 minutes. The Adjust button allows you to change the cooking time to 3 or 15 minutes. When using this button always quick-release the steam immediately after the timer beeps so as not to overcook the food.

Slow Cook button. This button allows the Instant Pot® to cook like a slow cooker. It defaults to a 4-hour cook time. The Adjust button allows you to change the temperature to Less, Normal, or More, which correspond to a slow cooker's low, normal, or high. The Plus and Minus buttons allow you to adjust the cooking time.

Keep Warm/Cancel button. When the Instant Pot® is being programmed or is in operation, pressing this button cancels the operation and returns the Instant Pot® to a standby state. When the Instant Pot® is in the standby state, pressing this button again activates the Keep Warm function.

Automatic Keep Warm function. After the ingredients in the Instant Pot® are finished cooking, the Instant Pot® automatically switches over to the Keep Warm function and will keep your food warm for up to 10 hours. This is perfect for soups, stews, and chili, allowing the spices and flavors to really marry for an even better taste. The first digit on the LED display will show an L to indicate that the Instant Pot® is in the

Keep Warm cycle, and the clock will count up from 0 seconds to 10 hours.

Timer button. This button allows you to delay the start of cooking up to 24 hours. After you select a cooking program and make any time adjustments, press the Timer button and use the Plus or Minus keys to enter the delayed hours; press the Timer button again and use the Plus or Minus keys to enter the delayed minutes. You can press the Keep Warm/Cancel button to cancel the timed delay. The Timer function doesn't work with the Sauté or Keep Warm functions.

Locking and Pressure-Release Methods

Other than the Sauté function, where the lid should be off, or the Slow Cook or Keep Warm functions, where the lid can be on or off, most of the cooking you'll do in the Instant Pot® will be under pressure, which means you need to know how to lock the lid before pressurized cooking and how to safely release the pressure after cooking. Once your ingredients are in the inner pot of the Instant Pot®, to lock the lid put the lid on the Instant Pot® with the triangle mark on the lid aligned with the Unlocked mark on the rim of the Instant Pot®. Then turn the lid 30 degrees clockwise until the triangle mark on the lid is aligned with the Locked mark on the rim. Turn the pointed end of the pressure release handle on top of the lid to the Sealing position. After your cooking program has ended or you've pressed the Keep Warm/Cancel button to end the cooking, there are two ways you can release the pressure:

Natural-release method. To naturally release the pressure, simply wait until the Instant Pot® has cooled sufficiently for all the pressure to be released and the float valve to drop, normally about 10–15 minutes. You can either unplug the Instant Pot® while the pressure naturally releases or allow the pressure to release while it is still on the Keep Warm function.

Quick-release method. The quick-release method stifles the cooking process and helps unlock the lid for immediate serving. To quickly release the pressure on the Instant Pot®, make sure you are wearing oven mitts, then turn the pressure release handle to the Venting position to let out steam until the float valve drops. This is generally not recommended for starchy items or large volumes of liquid (e.g., soup) so as to avoid any splattering that may occur. Be prepared, because the noise and geyser effect of the releasing steam during the quick-release method can be off-putting. Also, if you own dogs, apparently this release is the most frightening part of their day, so use caution.

Pot-in-Pot Accessories

Pot-in-pot cooking is when you place another cooking dish inside the Instant Pot® for a particular recipe. The Instant Pot® is straightforward and comes with an inner pot and trivet; however, many other tricks and recipes are made possible with the purchase of a few other accessories, including a springform pan, cake pan, glass bowl, and ramekins.

7" springform pan. A 7" springform pan is the perfect size for making a cheesecake in an Instant Pot®. It has the right dimensions to fit inside the Instant Pot®, and it makes a cheesecake for four to six people.

6" cake pan. A 6" cake pan is excellent for making a small cake in the Instant Pot®. It can serve four to six people depending on the serving size. This pan is perfect for a family craving a small dessert without committing to leftovers.

7-cup glass bowl. This 7-cup bowl fits perfectly on top of the trivet in the Instant Pot® and works great for eggs and bread puddings that generally would burn on the bottom of the pot insert. The items in the bowl sit up on the inserted trivet and are cooked with the steam and pressure of the pot.

Ramekins. These 4-ounce porcelain individual portions provide the perfect vessel for tasty custards.

Steamer basket. The steamer basket helps create a raised shelf for steaming. Shop around, as there are several variations, including metal or silicone steamer baskets. Some even have handles for ease of lifting after the cooking process.

Although these accessories help you branch out and make different recipes with the Instant Pot®, there are many recipes you can make using just the inner pot and trivet that come with your appliance. The accessories are just fun to use with what will soon become your favorite heat source in the kitchen.

Helpful Utensils

Cooking pot-in-pot is a great idea until it's time to remove the inserted cooking dish. Because of the tight space, it is almost impossible to use thick oven mitts to reach down and grip something evenly without tipping one side of the cooking vessel and spilling the cooked item. There are a few ways around this:

Retriever tongs. Retriever tongs are a helpful tool for removing hot bowls and pans from the Instant Pot®.

Mini mitts. Small silicone mitts are helpful when lifting inserts out of an Instant Pot® after the cooking process. They are less cumbersome than traditional oven mitts, which can prove to be bulky in the tight space of the cooker.

Aluminum foil sling. This is a quick, inexpensive fix to the problem of lifting a heated dish out of an Instant Pot®. Take a 10" × 10" square of aluminum foil and fold it back and forth until you have a 2" × 10" sling. Place this sling underneath the bowl or pan before cooking so that you can easily lift up the heated dish.

Although necessary if you do pot-in-pot cooking, these retrieval tools are not needed if you are simply using the interior pot that comes with the appliance upon purchase. A slotted spoon will do the trick for most other meals.

Cleaning Your Instant Pot®

When cleaning up after using your Instant Pot®, the first thing you should do is unplug the pot and allow it to cool. Then you can break down the following parts to clean and inspect for any trapped food particles:

Inner pot. The inner pot, the cooking vessel, is dishwasher-safe; however, the high heat causes rainbowing, or discoloration, on stainless steel. To avoid this, hand wash the pot.

Outer heating unit. Wipe the interior and exterior with a damp cloth. Do not submerge in water, as it is an electrical appliance.

Trivet. The trivet can be cleaned with soap and water or in the dishwasher.

Lid. The lid needs to be broken down into individual parts before washing. The sealing ring, the float valve, the steam release handle, and the antiblock shield all need to be cleaned in different ways.

- **Sealing ring.** Once this ring is removed, check the integrity of the silicone. If it is torn or cracked, it will not seal properly and may hinder the cooking process, in which case it should not be used. The sealing ring needs to be removed and washed each time because the ring has a tendency to hold odors when cooking. Vinegar or lemon juice is excellent for reducing odors. Additional rings can be purchased for a nominal price. Many Instant Pot® users buy more than one ring and use one for meats and a separate one for desserts and milder dishes.

- **Float valve.** The float valve is a safety feature that serves as a latch lock that prevents the lid from being opened during the cooking process. Make sure that this valve can move easily and is not obstructed by any food particles.

- **Pressure release handle.** This is the venting handle on top of the lid. It can be pulled out for cleaning. It should be loose, so don't worry. This allows it to move when necessary.

- **Antiblock shield.** The antiblock shield is the little silver "basket" underneath the lid. It is located directly below the vent. This shield can and should be removed and cleaned. It blocks any foods, especially starches, so they don't clog the vent.

So, now that you know about all the safety features, buttons, and parts of your Instant Pot® and know how to clean everything, it's time for the fun part. The cooking process is where the excitement begins. From breakfast to dessert and everything in between, the recipes in this book have you covered.

2

Breakfast and Brunch

Breakfast is the most important meal of the day, as they say. But a lot of people just don't have the time or energy to create a well-rounded plate of food. Most mornings you may just be too tired or too busy—or both. Fortunately, the Instant Pot® can help save the day with its shortened cooking time and freedom from having to stand over the skillet. All you have to do is add your ingredients, press a button, and go get ready to tackle your day. Try prepping some of the fruit and vegetables the night before so you can eliminate this step in the morning as well. And when breakfast is ready, all you have to do is drop the interior cooker pot right into your dishwasher, alleviating that hassle of coming home to a stack of dirty dishes.

This chapter has you covered with a myriad of delicious breakfast recipes, including Maple-Pecan Oatmeal, Poblano Hash Browns, and Three-Pepper Vegan Frittata. And once you get comfortable with some of the basics, you should feel free to get creative and make some of your own morning masterpieces!

Steel-Cut Oats

"Steel cut" refers to the chopping of whole oat kernels into two or three smaller pieces. The oats can then be further processed into rolled oats or prepared as is. These relatively unprocessed oats are high in B vitamins, calcium, protein, and fiber, but many cooks balk at the long prep time, typically 30 minutes or more. Instant Pot® cuts that in half—you'll have this healthiest of oatmeals ready to serve in 15 minutes flat!

- **Hands-On Time: 3 minutes**
- **Cook Time: 12 minutes**

Serves 2

4 cups water
1 cup steel-cut oats, toasted
1 tablespoon vegan
   margarine
Pinch salt

TOASTING STEEL-CUT OATS

To toast steel-cut oats, preheat the oven to 300°F. Place the oats on a large baking sheet. Bake 20 minutes. Store toasted steel-cut oats in a covered container in a cool place for up to 3–4 weeks. Toasting steel-cut oats will enhance the flavor and allow them to cook in approximately half the time.

1 In the Instant Pot®, combine all ingredients. Stir to combine and lock lid.

2 Press the Manual button and adjust time to 12 minutes. When the timer beeps, let pressure release naturally until float valve drops and then unlock lid.

3 Stir and then spoon the oats into serving bowls. Serve warm.

Banana Nut Bread Oatmeal

Once you've tasted this dish you'll no longer believe there is such a thing as an overripe banana. Savory and bursting with nuts and cinnamon, this reimagined banana bread is a delightful Instant Pot® oatmeal that's quick enough for a breakfast and delicious any time of day. The oats cook in 7 minutes, and it takes only a few minutes more to include the walnuts and pecans for taste, texture, and energy.

- **Hands-On Time: 5 minutes**
- **Cook Time: 7 minutes**

Serves 2

1 cup water

1 cup unsweetened soy milk or almond milk

1 cup old-fashioned oats

2 medium bananas, peeled and sliced

2 tablespoons light brown sugar

2 teaspoons ground cinnamon

2 tablespoons chopped walnuts

¼ teaspoon vanilla extract

Pinch salt

1   In the Instant Pot®, combine all ingredients. Stir to combine and lock lid.

2   Press the Manual button and adjust time to 7 minutes. When the timer beeps, let pressure release naturally until float valve drops and then unlock lid.

3   Stir oatmeal. Spoon the oats into serving bowls. Serve warm.

Apple Streusel Oatmeal

Though you might love to whip up a classic German streusel on your way out the door, chances are you don't quite get around to it. That's probably why so many of us have come to associate the dark, apple-sugar flavors of streusel with chalky instant-oatmeal-in-a-pouch. This scratch recipe, ready in 15 minutes, will take care of that. Sweet, savory, and packed with fruit and nuts, this divine Instant Pot® breakfast isn't (quite) as decadent as it sounds.

- **Hands-On Time: 5 minutes**
- **Cook Time: 8 minutes**

Serves 2

1 cup water

1 cup unsweetened soy milk or almond milk

1 cup old-fashioned oats

2 medium Granny Smith apples, peeled, cored, and diced

2 tablespoons light brown sugar

2 teaspoons ground cinnamon

2 tablespoons chopped pecans

1 In the Instant Pot®, combine the water, soy milk, oats, apples, brown sugar, and cinnamon. Stir to combine and lock lid.

2 Press the Manual button and adjust time to 8 minutes. When the timer beeps, let pressure release naturally until float valve drops and then unlock lid.

3 Stir the oatmeal. Spoon the oats into serving bowls and top with pecans. Serve warm.

Irish Oatmeal with Fruit

Steel-cut oats have gone mainstream in recent years, but it's the same cut we've long known as Irish oatmeal. Let this recipe serve as a foundation and add whatever dried fruit you have on hand. Raisins, dates, and cherries are traditional favorites.

- **Hands-On Time: 5 minutes**
- **Cook Time: 10 minutes**

Serves 2

2 cups water

1 cup old-fashioned oats, toasted

2 teaspoons vegan margarine

1 cup apple juice

1 tablespoon dried cranberries

1 tablespoon golden raisins

1 tablespoon chopped dried apricots

1 tablespoon maple syrup

¼ teaspoon ground cinnamon

Pinch salt

1 In the Instant Pot®, combine the water, oats, margarine, apple juice, cranberries, raisins, apricots, maple syrup, cinnamon, and salt. Stir to combine and lock lid.

2 Press the Manual button and adjust time to 10 minutes. When the timer beeps, let pressure release naturally until float valve drops and then unlock lid.

3 Stir oatmeal. Spoon the oats into serving bowls. Serve warm.

COOKING AHEAD

If you're not a morning person, you can make Irish Oatmeal with Fruit the night before. Once it's cooled, divide between two covered microwave-safe containers and refrigerate overnight. The next morning, cover each bowl with a paper towel to catch any splatters and then microwave on high 1–2 minutes or until heated through.

Maple-Pecan Oatmeal

This traditional oatmeal calls for old-fashioned rolled oats—most oatmeal aficionados would insist—but the quick-cooking variety will do in a pinch. If you do substitute, remember to adjust cooking time accordingly, in this case by about half.

- **Hands-On Time: 5 minutes**
- **Cook Time: 7 minutes**

Serves 2

1 cup water
1 cup unsweetened soy milk or almond milk
1 cup old-fashioned oats
2 tablespoons maple syrup
2 tablespoons chopped pecans

1 In the Instant Pot®, combine the water, soy milk, oats, and maple syrup. Stir to combine and lock lid.

2 Press the Manual button and adjust time to 7 minutes. When the timer beeps, let pressure release naturally until float valve drops and then unlock lid.

3 Stir oatmeal. Spoon the oats into serving bowls and top with pecans. Serve warm.

Grits

Grits—the ground cornmeal dish synonymous with the American South—are simple, aromatic, and greatly improved by pressure cooking, making them an Instant Pot® showpiece. You'll find that slowly adding grits to boiling water while gently stirring will help prevent clumping.

- **Hands-On Time: 5 minutes**
- **Cook Time: 10 minutes**

Serves 4

2¼ cups water, divided
1 cup stone-ground grits
2 tablespoons vegan margarine
1 teaspoon salt
½ teaspoon freshly ground black pepper

1 Add ¾ cup water to the Instant Pot®. Insert the trivet.

2 In the stainless steel bowl that fits into the pot insert, stir together the remaining water, grits, margarine, salt, and pepper. Lock lid.

3 Press the Rice button and adjust the timer to 10 minutes. When the timer beeps, quick-release the pressure until the float valve drops and then unlock the lid. Serve warm.

Red Pepper Grits

Cooking grits in vegetable broth instead of water adds depth to the flavor and makes this ingredient more appropriate for dinner or lunch. These Red Pepper Grits are hot and spicy, which gives them a different character than traditional grits.

- **Hands-On Time: 5 minutes**
- **Cook Time: 10 minutes**

Serves 4

¾ cup water
1 cup stone-ground grits
¼ cup vegan margarine
4 cups vegetable broth
1 teaspoon salt
¼ teaspoon dried thyme
½ tablespoon dried red pepper flakes

1 Add the water to the Instant Pot®. Insert the trivet.

2 In the stainless steel bowl that fits into the pot insert, stir together the grits, margarine, broth, salt, and thyme. Lock the lid.

3 Press the Rice button and adjust the timer to 10 minutes. When the timer beeps, quick-release the pressure until the float valve drops and then unlock the lid.

4 Stir the red pepper flakes into the grits. Serve warm.

Cornmeal Mush

Let your Instant Pot® help you say good morning to mush. If you prefer your mush sweetened, you can add maple syrup or your sweetener of choice.

- **Hands-On Time: 5 minutes**
- **Cook Time: 15 minutes**

Serves 6

1 cup yellow cornmeal
4 cups water, divided
½ teaspoon salt
1 tablespoon vegan margarine

1 In a medium bowl, whisk together the cornmeal, 1 cup water, and salt. Set aside.

2 Add the remaining water to the Instant Pot®, press the Sauté button, and adjust to High. Bring to a boil. Stir the cornmeal and water mixture into the boiling water. Add the margarine and stir continuously until the mixture returns to a boil.

3 Lock the lid into place. Press the Manual button and adjust time to 10 minutes. When the timer beeps, quick-release the pressure until the float valve drops and then unlock the lid.

4 Spoon into serving bowls and serve warm.

Spicy Tofu Scramble

A spiced-up take on the classic tofu scramble, this dish pairs perfectly with a traditional Mexican breakfast of beans and rice and wraps right up as a breakfast burrito. Balance the flavors a bit with avocado slices or a dollop of vegan sour cream. And be warned: as described here, this dish is one of the spiciest in this book!

- **Hands-On Time: 10 minutes**
- **Cook Time: 14 minutes**

Serves 2

16 ounces firm tofu, drained
1 teaspoon fresh lemon juice
1 teaspoon salt
½ teaspoon freshly ground
   black pepper
½ teaspoon turmeric powder
1 tablespoon olive oil
¼ cup diced red onion
¼ cup diced red bell pepper
¼ cup diced tomato
1 clove garlic, minced
1 teaspoon ground cumin
½ teaspoon chipotle powder
½ teaspoon chili powder
¼ cup water
2 tablespoons chopped fresh
   cilantro

1 In a large bowl, mash the tofu with your hands or a fork, then stir in the lemon juice, salt, pepper, and turmeric.

2 Add the olive oil to the Instant Pot® and select the Sauté button. Add the onion and bell pepper; sauté 3 minutes. Add the tomato, garlic, cumin, chipotle powder, and chili powder; sauté an additional 30 seconds.

3 Add the tofu mixture and water to the pot and stir. Lock the lid into place, press the Manual button, and adjust time to 10 minutes. When the timer beeps, let pressure release naturally until float valve drops and then unlock lid.

4 Stir in the cilantro and spoon the scramble into serving bowls. Serve warm.

Hash Browns

Let Waffle House inspire you and serve these hash browns any way you'd like—scattered, covered, or smothered. This is another fine task for your Instant Pot®, because as any home breakfast chef knows, hash browns prepared the traditional way are endlessly tricky.

- **Hands-On Time: 5 minutes**
- **Cook Time: 15 minutes**

Serves 4

2 tablespoons olive oil

2 tablespoons vegan margarine

4 cups peeled and grated russet potatoes

Pinch salt

Pinch freshly ground black pepper

PREPARING THE POTATOES

Rinsing and thoroughly drying the grated potatoes will help you achieve a delicious crispy brown exterior on your hash browns. After grating the potatoes, pour them into a colander and let them sit under running cold water for 1 minute. Drain the potatoes and let them air-dry for 10–30 minutes, or use a towel to remove excess water before cooking.

1 Add the oil and margarine to the Instant Pot® and press the Sauté button. Add the potatoes and sauté 5 minutes, stirring occasionally, until they just begin to brown.

2 Season with salt and pepper. Use a wide spatula to press down firmly on the potatoes in the pot.

3 Lock the lid into place. Press the Manual button and adjust time to 10 minutes. When the timer beeps, quick-release the pressure until the float valve drops and then unlock the lid. Serve warm.

Garden Tofu Scramble

A go-to tofu scramble is a staple in any vegan kitchen, and your Instant Pot® makes a good thing even better. Try this one as presented until you're comfortable with the steps and timing, then riff away. One good way to start your experimenting: substitute shiitake mushrooms and Japanese eggplant for the button mushrooms and broccoli.

- **Hands-On Time: 10 minutes**
- **Cook Time: 15 minutes**

Serves 2

16 ounces firm tofu, drained
1 teaspoon fresh lemon juice
1 teaspoon salt
½ teaspoon freshly ground black pepper
½ teaspoon turmeric powder
1 tablespoon olive oil
½ cup broccoli florets, blanched
½ cup sliced button mushrooms
½ cup diced tomato
1 clove garlic, minced
¼ cup water
2 tablespoons chopped fresh Italian flat-leaf parsley

1 In a large bowl, mash the tofu with your hands or a fork, then stir in the lemon juice, salt, pepper, and turmeric.

2 Add the olive oil to the Instant Pot® and press the Sauté button. Add the broccoli and mushrooms and sauté 4–5 minutes. Add the tomato and garlic and sauté an additional 30 seconds.

3 Add the tofu mixture and water to the pot and stir. Lock the lid into place, press the Manual button, and adjust the timer to 10 minutes. When the timer beeps, let pressure release naturally until float valve drops and then unlock lid.

4 Stir in the parsley and spoon the scramble into serving bowls. Serve warm.

Poblano Hash Browns

Any type of pepper will do for this slightly spicy take on hash browns, so try poblano, jalapeño, or bell peppers to your taste. Another option: take the spice to the next level with ¼ teaspoon of cayenne pepper and a bit of extra cumin.

- **Hands-On Time: 5 minutes**
- **Cook Time: 16 minutes**

Serves 4

2 tablespoons olive oil

2 tablespoons vegan margarine

4 cups peeled and grated russet potatoes

¼ cup diced yellow onion

1 poblano pepper, cored, seeded, and diced

1 clove garlic, minced

Pinch salt

Pinch freshly ground black pepper

1 teaspoon ground cumin

1 Add the oil and margarine to the Instant Pot® and press the Sauté button.

2 Add the potatoes, onion, and poblano pepper. Sauté 5 minutes, stirring occasionally, until the potatoes just begin to brown. Add the garlic and sauté 30 seconds.

3 Season with the salt, pepper, and cumin. Use a wide spatula to press down firmly on the potatoes in the pan.

4 Lock the lid into place. Press the Manual button and adjust time to 10 minutes. When the timer beeps, quick-release the pressure until the float valve drops and then unlock the lid. Serve warm.

Home Fries

Who needs a live-in chef when you have an Instant Pot®, which never asks for a morning off and can whip up home fries in 15 minutes? Some cooks disavow paprika with the claim that it adds little to no flavor to a dish after cooking. This is debatable and depends on portions—either way, in many dishes such as this one, the paprika is as much about color as flavor. Use it!

- **Hands-On Time: 5 minutes**
- **Cook Time: 15 minutes**

Serves 4

2 tablespoons olive oil
4 cups diced red potatoes
1½ teaspoons paprika
1 teaspoon chili powder
1½ teaspoons salt
1 teaspoon freshly ground
   black pepper

1 Add the oil to the Instant Pot® and press the Sauté button.

2 Add the potatoes and sauté 3–5 minutes, stirring occasionally. Add all remaining ingredients and stir.

3 Lock the lid into place. Press the Manual button and adjust time to 10 minutes. When the timer beeps, quick-release the pressure until the float valve drops and then unlock the lid. Serve warm.

Three-Pepper Vegan Frittata

The Instant Pot® does wonders with firm tofu for a cholesterol-free breakfast frittata. Remember here that a frittata is similar to an omelet, so you should feel at liberty to experiment with slightly shorter or longer cooking times.

- **Hands-On Time: 10 minutes**
- **Cook Time: 12 minutes**

Serves 4

16 ounces firm tofu, drained
½ cup unsweetened soy milk
4 teaspoons cornstarch
2 teaspoons nutritional yeast
1 teaspoon spicy mustard
½ teaspoon turmeric powder
1 teaspoon salt
2 tablespoons olive oil
1 cup peeled and diced red potatoes
½ cup diced red onion
½ cup diced red bell pepper
½ cup diced green bell pepper
1 teaspoon minced jalapeño pepper
1 clove garlic, minced
¼ cup chopped fresh Italian flat-leaf parsley
¾ cup water

1. In a blender or food processor combine the tofu, soy milk, cornstarch, nutritional yeast, mustard, turmeric, and salt and process until smooth. Set aside.

2. Add the olive oil to the Instant Pot® and press the Sauté button. Add the potatoes, onion, peppers, garlic, and parsley; sauté 3–5 minutes.

3. Transfer the cooked mixture to a 7-cup greased glass dish and pour the tofu mixture into the cooked potato mixture.

4. Place the trivet in the Instant Pot®. Pour in the water. Place the dish with the tofu mixture on the trivet. Lock the lid into place. Press the Manual button and adjust time to 7 minutes. When the timer beeps, let pressure release naturally until the float valve drops and then unlock lid.

5. Remove the dish from the pot and put aside 5–10 minutes to set. Slice and serve.

MAKE IT A SCRAMBLE
To shorten the preparation time for this meal while keeping all the flavors, try making this dish into a scramble by preparing the entire recipe in the Instant Pot®. Skip the step of blending the tofu and omit the cornstarch.

Yeasty Tofu and Veggies

Remember that nutritional yeast has a cheesy flavor that is not easily substituted with other yeasts. As long as you have some on hand, this is one of the quickest start-to-finish meals you'll prepare with your Instant Pot®. As (almost) always, the vegetables here are suggestions; just be sure to adjust your sauté time accordingly.

- **Hands-On Time: 25 minutes**
- **Cook Time: 17 minutes**

Serves 4

16 ounces extra-firm tofu, drained

2 tablespoons vegetable oil, divided

2 tablespoons soy sauce, divided

1 cup water

½ medium red onion, peeled and diced

1 cup chopped broccoli, blanched

½ medium green bell pepper, seeded and chopped

½ medium zucchini, chopped

½ cup chopped yellow squash

¼ cup nutritional yeast

1 Wrap the block of tofu in paper towels and place a heavy plate on top; let sit 5 minutes. Remove the paper towels and cut the tofu into ½"-thick pieces.

2 Add 1 tablespoon oil to the Instant Pot® and press the Sauté button. Sauté the tofu 7 minutes until light brown on all sides. Add 1 tablespoon soy sauce and sauté 10 seconds more. Remove the tofu and set aside.

3 Add the remaining oil to the pot along with the water, onions, broccoli, bell pepper, zucchini, and squash; sauté 10 minutes until tender. Add the tofu and remaining soy sauce and sauté 1 minute more. Sprinkle the nutritional yeast on top and serve.

Spinach and Portobello Benedict

Though its fancy name, meaty texture, and earthy flavor might fool you, the portobello is just a type of mature common mushroom, and it can be substituted with cooking-time adjustments in any recipe that calls for them. For this and any other recipe, vegans should be sure to check the label before purchasing English muffins, as some brands are made with animal products.

- **Hands-On Time: 10 minutes**
- **Cook Time: 15 minutes**

Serves 2

½ cup silken tofu
1 tablespoon fresh lemon juice
1 teaspoon Dijon mustard
⅛ teaspoon cayenne pepper
⅛ teaspoon turmeric powder
1 tablespoon vegetable oil
Pinch salt
1 tablespoon olive oil
4 small portobello mushroom caps
2 cups fresh spinach leaves
2 vegan English muffins, toasted

1 Add the silken tofu to a food processor and purée until smooth. Add the lemon juice, mustard, cayenne, and turmeric. Blend until well combined. With the food processor still running, slowly add the vegetable oil and blend until combined. Season with salt to complete the vegan hollandaise.

2 Pour the hollandaise into a small saucepan and heat on low. Keep warm until ready to serve.

3 Press the Sauté button on the Instant Pot® and add the olive oil. Add the mushroom caps and spinach and stir until coated with the oil and slightly softened, about 3 minutes.

4 Lock the lid into place. Press the Manual button and adjust time to 9 minutes. When the timer beeps, let pressure release naturally until the float valve drops and then unlock lid.

5 Place a toasted English muffin open-faced on each plate and top each half with a Portobello cap and sautéed spinach. Drizzle with a spoonful of the warm vegan hollandaise to finish.

Tofu Ranchero

This Southwestern breakfast classic is a vessel ready for the salsa and condiments of your choice. If you find that firm tofu isn't quite firm enough for your taste, go for extra-firm. Don't use anything less than firm, though, as it is unlikely it will stand up properly to cooking.

- **Hands-On Time: 10 minutes**
- **Cook Time: 20 minutes**

Serves 4

16 ounces firm tofu, drained

1 teaspoon fresh lemon juice

1 teaspoon salt

½ teaspoon freshly ground black pepper

½ teaspoon turmeric powder

2 tablespoons olive oil, divided

¼ cup diced red onion

1 clove garlic, minced

8 (10") corn tortillas

1 cup vegetarian refried beans, warmed

½ cup shredded vegan Cheddar cheese

½ cup chipotle salsa

CHOOSING SALSA

Salsa comes in many delicious and unique varieties. Most are clearly labeled mild, medium, and hot, but one's interpretation of those words can vary greatly. Chipotle salsa has a deep, earthy spice, but you can also use plain tomato salsa in this recipe.

1 Preheat the oven to 350°F.

2 In a large bowl, mash the tofu with your hands or a fork, then stir in the lemon juice, salt, pepper, and turmeric.

3 Add 1 tablespoon olive oil to the Instant Pot® and press the Sauté button. Add the onion and sauté 3 minutes. Add the garlic and sauté 30 seconds.

4 Stir in the tofu mixture, then lock the lid into place. Press the Manual button and adjust the timer to 10 minutes. When the timer beeps, quick-release the pressure until the float valve drops.

5 Heat the remaining oil in a small sauté pan over medium heat. Heat the tortillas one at a time until they begin to puff up slightly, about 30 seconds per side.

6 Lay out the tortillas on one or two baking sheets to allow for size. Divide the refried beans evenly among the tortillas. Top with the cooked tofu mixture and sprinkle cheese evenly over each tortilla. Bake 2 minutes or until the cheese melts.

7 Remove from the oven and top with salsa before serving.

Breakfast Burrito

Some prefer extra-firm tofu for dishes like this one—it's a matter of preference and taste, though going any softer than the firm variety leads to a very thin consistency and is not recommended. Adjust the Instant Pot® sautéing time accordingly.

- **Hands-On Time: 10 minutes**
- **Cook Time: 12 minutes**

Serves 4

2 tablespoons olive oil

16 ounces firm tofu, drained and diced

¼ cup diced red onion

½ cup diced tomato

¼ cup chopped fresh cilantro

¼ cup water

1 teaspoon salt

4 (10") flour tortillas

1 cup canned black beans, warmed

1 medium avocado, peeled and sliced

½ cup vegan sour cream (optional)

½ cup shredded vegan Cheddar cheese (optional)

STEAMING TORTILLAS

For best results, steam tortillas on the stovetop using a steamer basket. If you're in a hurry, throw the tortillas into the microwave one at a time and heat for about 30 seconds.

1 Add the oil to the Instant Pot® and press the Sauté button. Add the tofu, stir until well coated, and sauté until it begins to brown, about 5 minutes. Add the onion, tomato, cilantro, water, and salt.

2 Lock the lid into place. Press the Manual button and adjust time to 7 minutes. When the timer beeps, let pressure release naturally until the float valve drops and then unlock lid.

3 Steam or microwave the tortillas until softened, then lay the tortillas on a flat surface to build the burritos. Place equal amounts of the tofu mixture, beans, and avocado in a line down the center of each tortilla.

4 Roll each burrito by first folding the sides of the tortilla over the filling. Then, while still holding the sides closed, fold the bottom of the tortilla over the filling. Next, roll the burrito while still holding the sides closed and pushing the filling down into the burrito if it starts to spill out. Repeat for remaining burritos.

5 Top with vegan sour cream and/or vegan cheese if desired.

Breakfast Casserole

Casserole is a French word that developed from the Provençal word for "pan." And yes, even casseroles can be made in an Instant Pot®! The proteins in this Breakfast Casserole are suggestions, of course, and many vegan cheeses and meat substitutes or even mushrooms can be employed to delicious effect.

- **Hands-On Time: 5 minutes**
- **Cook Time: 17 minutes**

Serves 4

2 tablespoons vegetable oil

1 medium yellow onion, peeled and diced

½ medium green bell pepper, seeded and chopped

1 (8-ounce) package vegan sausage crumbles

3 cups peeled and shredded russet potatoes

16 ounces firm tofu, crumbled

2 cups vegan Cheddar cheese

Pinch salt

Pinch freshly ground black pepper

1 Select Sauté on the Instant Pot® and add the oil. Add the onion and bell pepper and sauté 3–5 minutes until tender. Add the sausage and cook 2–3 minutes until heated through. Add the remaining ingredients and stir to combine.

2 Lock the lid into place. Press the Manual button and adjust time to 9 minutes. When the timer beeps, let pressure release naturally until the float valve drops and then unlock lid. Serve warm.

3

Appetizers and Snacks

Appetizers are a great way to bring a group of people together to enjoy a game or hold them over until you serve a meal. But you don't want to have to wear your chef hat all day, stuck in the kitchen, so let the Instant Pot® be your kitchen helper. Warm, delicious food in minutes? Now that's how you throw a party! With amazing appetizers ranging from Wasabi-Barbecue Chickpeas and Black Bean Dip to Texas Caviar, the only problem you'll have incorporating the recipes in this chapter into your next social event will be deciding which one to cook.

Wheat Berry Salad

For an elegant presentation that makes a great opening or even a nice quick bite between courses, place a teaspoon of Wheat Berry Salad on individual sections of baby romaine hearts. If you're pinched for time, you can scale back the impressive ingredient list and still emerge with a bright, fresh salad.

- **Hands-On Time: 15 minutes**
- **Cook Time: 40 minutes**

Serves 12

1½ tablespoons vegetable oil
6¾ cups water
1½ cups wheat berries
1½ teaspoons Dijon mustard
1 teaspoon granulated sugar
1 teaspoon sea salt
½ teaspoon freshly ground
    black pepper
¼ cup white wine vinegar
½ cup extra-virgin olive oil
½ small red onion, peeled
    and diced
1⅓ cups frozen corn or peas,
    thawed
1 medium zucchini, peeled,
    grated, and drained
2 medium stalks celery, finely
    diced
1 medium red bell pepper,
    seeded and diced
4 green onions, diced
¼ cup sun-dried tomatoes,
    diced
¼ cup chopped fresh Italian
    flat-leaf parsley

1 Press the Multigrain button on the Instant Pot® and add the vegetable oil, water, and wheat berries. Lock the lid into place and set the timer for the default time of 40 minutes. When the timer beeps, quick-release the pressure until the float valve drops and then unlock the lid. Fluff the wheat berries with a fork. If the grains aren't as tender as you'd like, press the Sauté button on the pot and simmer the mixture for a few minutes, stirring and adding more water if necessary. When done to your liking, drain and transfer to a large bowl.

2 Make the dressing by puréeing the mustard, sugar, salt, pepper, vinegar, olive oil, and red onion in a food processor or blender until smooth.

3 Stir ½ cup dressing into the cooled wheat berries. Toss the seasoned wheat berries with the remaining ingredients.

4 Taste for seasoning and add additional salt, pepper, or dressing if desired. Cover and refrigerate any leftover dressing up to 3 days.

Tomato, Garlic, and Parsley Quinoa Salad

The Mediterranean combination of tomato, garlic, and parsley goes well with just about any grain, so if you're not in a quinoa mood, try couscous or even rice instead. Just make sure you double back and give this quinoa recipe a try, as the texture here is hard to beat.

- **Hands-On Time: 5 minutes**
- **Cook Time: 22 minutes**

Serves 4

2 tablespoons olive oil
2 cloves garlic, minced
1 cup diced tomatoes
¼ cup chopped fresh Italian flat-leaf parsley
1 tablespoon fresh lemon juice
1 cup quinoa
2 cups water
1 teaspoon salt

1 Press the Sauté button on the Instant Pot® and add the olive oil. Sauté the garlic 30 seconds, then add the tomatoes, parsley, and lemon juice. Sauté an additional minute. Transfer the tomato mixture to a small bowl.

2 Press the Multigrain button on the Instant Pot® and add the quinoa and water. Lock the lid into place. and adjust the timer to 20 minutes. When the timer beeps, let pressure release naturally until float valve drops and then unlock lid. Fluff with a fork.

3 Stir the tomato mixture and salt into the cooked quinoa in the pot. Season with additional salt if desired and serve immediately.

Three Bean Salad

This light salad—as much a vehicle for apple cider vinegar as for the beans themselves—is made to be served chilled, so cover and refrigerate for at least 2 hours before serving. It can even be made a day in advance and left in the refrigerator overnight.

- **Hands-On Time: 5 minutes**
- **Cook Time: 30 minutes**

Serves 8

⅓ cup apple cider vinegar
¼ cup granulated sugar
2½ teaspoons salt, divided
½ teaspoon freshly ground black pepper
¼ cup olive oil
½ cup dried chickpeas
½ cup dried kidney beans
1 cup frozen green beans pieces (about 1" pieces)
4 cups water
1 tablespoon vegetable oil
1 cup chopped fresh Italian flat-leaf parsley
½ cup diced red onion
½ cup peeled and diced cucumber

1 **For the dressing:** In a small bowl, whisk together the vinegar, sugar, 1½ teaspoons salt, and pepper. While whisking continuously, slowly add the olive oil. Once well combined, cover and refrigerate.

2 Add the chickpeas, kidney beans, green beans, water, vegetable oil, and remaining salt to the Instant Pot®. Stir to combine. Lock the lid into place, press the Bean button, and cook for the default time of 30 minutes.

3 When the timer beeps, let pressure release naturally for 10 minutes. Quick-release any remaining pressure until float valve drops and then unlock lid.

4 Transfer the cooked beans to a large mixing bowl. Stir in all remaining ingredients and dressing, and toss to combine thoroughly. Cover and refrigerate 2 hours before serving.

BEAN VARIATIONS
Almost any combination of beans can be used to make a bean salad. Try black beans, pinto beans, and navy beans mixed with Mexican flavors, or adzuki beans, soybeans, and green beans with Japanese flavors.

Olive and Pepper Couscous Salad

Black kalamata olives add a deep savory flavor to this Olive and Pepper Couscous Salad and are recommended over most other varieties here. One exception: for a similar flavor with a bit less olive in the bite, try the larger-pitted Nicoise olive.

- **Hands-On Time: 5 minutes**
- **Cook Time: 7 minutes**

Serves 4

1 cup couscous
2 cups water
½ cup mixed olives, pitted and chopped
1 medium red bell pepper, seeded and diced
1 clove garlic, minced
1 teaspoon olive oil
1 teaspoon red wine vinegar
1 teaspoon salt

1 Stir together the couscous and water in the Instant Pot®. Press the Manual button, adjust timer to 7 minutes, and lock the lid into place. When the timer beeps, let pressure release naturally until float valve drops and then unlock lid.

2 Fluff the couscous with a fork. Add all remaining ingredients and stir until combined.

3 Refrigerate 2 hours before serving.

Couscous-Stuffed Red Peppers

Pine nuts are also called pinoli or pignoli, and are most commonly known for being a key ingredient in pesto. Couscous is a perfect Instant Pot® dish, as the pressure infuses the grain with flavor in ways traditional preparation doesn't match. Pine nut prices have soared in recent years—many cooks substitute slivered almonds when necessary for this reason.

- **Hands-On Time: 5 minutes**
- **Cook Time: 23 minutes**

Serves 4

1 cup couscous

2 cups water

2 tablespoons pine nuts

4 ounces crumbled vegan feta, such as Sunergia Soy Feta Cheese

1 teaspoon dried oregano

1 teaspoon salt

4 large red bell peppers, stemmed and cored

PEPPER PEAK SEASON
Peppers are available in most grocery stores year-round, but red peppers are at their best during the summer months.

1 Preheat the oven to 350°F.

2 Add the couscous and water to the Instant Pot®. Lock the lid into place, press the Manual button, and adjust the timer to 6 minutes. When the timer beeps, let pressure release naturally until float valve drops and then unlock lid.

3 While the couscous is cooking, toast the pine nuts in a small sauté pan over low heat, stirring often to avoid burning. Once they begin to turn golden brown, remove from heat.

4 Fluff the couscous and add the pine nuts, feta, oregano, and salt. Stir well to combine.

5 Stuff ¼ of the couscous mixture into each bell pepper and place in an ungreased baking dish. Bake 15 minutes or until the peppers begin to soften.

Cranberry-Pecan Pilaf

Like most cranberry-pecan concoctions, this pilaf calls to mind a golden autumn afternoon, but it makes for a great light dish any time of year. To bring more flavors into this dish, try sprinkling in ginger or cloves, and to make this a complete meal, add vegan beef, such as Gardein Beefless Tips.

- **Hands-On Time: 5 minutes**
- **Cook Time: 30 minutes**

Serves 4

1 cup long-grain white rice
2 cups vegetable broth
⅔ cup dried cranberries
1 teaspoon dried thyme
1 bay leaf
1 cup pecan pieces
2 tablespoons vegan margarine
Pinch salt
Pinch freshly ground black pepper

1. Add the rice, broth, cranberries, thyme, and bay leaf to the Instant Pot® and press the Rice button. Let the timer set for the default time. Lock the lid into place. When the timer beeps, let pressure release naturally until float valve drops and then unlock lid.

2. Discard the bay leaf and stir in the pecans, margarine, salt, and pepper. Serve warm.

SERVING SUGGESTIONS
Turn this pilaf into a holiday dinner centerpiece by serving it in a cooked acorn squash or small pumpkin.

Creamy Thyme Polenta

Is there such a thing as polenta that's not creamy? Give this recipe a try and you'll see why we named it this way. To substitute fresh thyme, increase the portion to 1 tablespoon. This is the rule for all such conversions: 1 part dried herb requires 3 parts fresh as a replacement, and vice versa.

- **Hands-On Time: 5 minutes**
- **Cook Time: 10 minutes**

Serves 4

3½ cups water
½ cup coarse polenta
½ cup fine yellow cornmeal
1 cup corn kernels
1 teaspoon dried thyme
1 teaspoon salt

1 In the Instant Pot®, stir together all ingredients. Press the Manual button, adjust the timer to 10 minutes, and lock the lid into place. When the timer beeps, quick-release the pressure until the float-valve drops and then unlock the lid.

2 Season with additional salt if desired, and serve warm.

Sea Salt Edamame

Edamame is a traditional Japanese preparation of baby soybeans that has migrated to the cuisines of China, Korea, Hawaii, and more recently to the rest of the world. The serving salt is optional, as the original Japanese dish omits it.

- **Hands-On Time: 5 minutes**
- **Cook Time: 25 minutes**

Serves 4

1 cup shelled edamame
4 cups water
1 tablespoon vegetable oil
1 teaspoon coarse sea salt
1 tablespoon soy sauce

1 Add the edamame, water, and oil to the Instant Pot® and stir to combine thoroughly. Lock the lid into place, press the Bean button, and adjust the timer to 25 minutes.

2 When the timer beeps, let pressure release naturally for 10 minutes. Quick-release any remaining pressure until float valve drops and then unlock lid.

3 Drain the edamame and transfer to a serving bowl. Sprinkle with salt and serve with soy sauce on the side for dipping.

Quick Single-Serve Paella

While the rest of the world tends to consider paella Spain's national dish, the cooks of Valencia take special pride in this nineteenth-century creation, and their fellow Spaniards respect its Valencian origin. Turmeric is a budget-friendly alternative to saffron here, but primarily as a colorant. If you do have saffron on hand, increase the portion to 1 tablespoon.

- **Hands-On Time: 10 minutes**
- **Cook Time: 14 minutes**

Serves 4

3 tablespoons olive oil

1 medium sweet onion, peeled and chopped

1 cup peeled and grated carrot

1 medium red bell pepper, seeded and chopped

1 cup fresh or frozen green peas

1 clove garlic, minced

1 cup basmati rice

1½ teaspoons turmeric powder

2 cups vegetable broth

¼ cup chopped fresh Italian flat-leaf parsley

Pinch salt

Pinch freshly ground black pepper

1   Press the Sauté button on the Instant Pot®. Add the olive oil and sauté the onion, carrot, bell pepper, and peas until they begin to soften, about 5 minutes. Add the garlic, rice, and turmeric, and stir until well coated.

2   Add the broth and parsley. Lock the lid into place, press the Manual button, and adjust the timer to 9 minutes. When the timer beeps, let pressure release naturally until float valve drops and then unlock lid.

3   Season with salt and pepper before serving.

PAELLA STAPLES

There aren't many right or wrong ingredients for paella because it comes in many varieties. The two ingredients that are consistently used are rice and saffron (or turmeric).

White Beans with Garlic and Fresh Tomato

Cherry or Roma tomatoes work best for this recipe, but any variety will do in a pinch. At the risk of breaking the romantic spell that helps make them so popular, we'll let you in on a not-so-secret fact: nearly all Roma tomatoes sold in the US trace to a tomato developed in Maryland in the 1950s.

- **Hands-On Time: 5 minutes**
- **Cook Time: 40 minutes**

Serves 4

1 cup dried cannellini beans
4 cups vegetable broth
1 tablespoon vegetable oil
1 teaspoon salt
2 cloves garlic, minced
½ cup diced tomato
½ teaspoon dried sage
½ teaspoon freshly ground
  black pepper

1 Add the beans, broth, oil, and salt to the Instant Pot®, and stir all ingredients until thoroughly combined. Lock the lid into place. Press the Bean button and cook for default time of 30 minutes.

2 When the timer beeps, let pressure release naturally for 10 minutes. Quick-release any remaining pressure until float valve drops and then unlock lid.

3 Press the Sauté button and then press the Adjust button to change the temperature to Less. Add the remaining ingredients and simmer uncovered 10 minutes until thickened.

Texas Caviar

This is a great dish and worth the effort to plan ahead so that it can be served chilled. Prepare up to 2 days in advance and store in a covered container in the refrigerator. Texas Caviar is said to have first been served on New Year's Eve at the Houston Country Club sometime around 1940.

- **Hands-On Time: 5 minutes**
- **Cook Time: 30 minutes**

Yields 5 cups

1 cup dried black-eyed peas
4 cups water
1 pound cooked corn kernels
½ medium red onion, peeled and diced
½ medium green bell pepper, seeded and diced
1 pickled jalapeño, finely chopped
1 medium tomato, diced
2 tablespoons chopped fresh cilantro
¼ cup red wine vinegar
2 tablespoons extra-virgin olive oil
1 teaspoon salt
½ teaspoon freshly ground black pepper
½ teaspoon ground cumin

1 Press the Bean button on the Instant Pot® and add the black-eyed peas and water. Lock the lid into place and cook for the default time of 30 minutes.

2 When the timer beeps, allow pressure to release naturally until float valve drops and unlock lid. Drain the peas.

3 Transfer the peas to a large mixing bowl. Add all remaining ingredients to the beans and stir until thoroughly combined.

4 Refrigerate 1–2 hours before serving.

White Bean–Leek Purée

Tarragon is a pungent herb that isn't to everyone's taste. If you're not familiar with it, take a sniff before using tarragon here. If it seems a bit strong, replace it with sage in this recipe, or substitute more garlic and some ginger instead.

- **Hands-On Time: 10 minutes**
- **Cook Time: 40 minutes**

Serves 4

1 cup dried cannellini beans

5 cups vegetable broth, divided

1 tablespoon vegetable oil

½ teaspoon salt

1 cup thinly sliced leeks

1 teaspoon fresh lemon juice

2 cloves garlic, minced

¼ teaspoon dried tarragon

1 Add the beans, 4 cups broth, oil, and salt to the Instant Pot®, and stir until thoroughly combined. Lock the lid into place. Press the Bean button and cook for default time of 30 minutes.

2 When the timer beeps, let pressure release naturally for 10 minutes. Quick-release any remaining pressure until float valve drops and then unlock lid.

3 Press the Sauté button and then press the Adjust button to change the temperature to Less. Add the leeks, lemon juice, garlic, and tarragon and simmer uncovered 10 minutes to thicken.

4 Pour the bean mixture and remaining 1 cup broth into a large food processor or blender and blend until creamy. Season with additional salt if desired.

Wasabi-Barbecue Chickpeas

Bottled barbecue sauces in your local grocery store will tend to be vegan, because most are spicy ketchup in one form or another. Some do contain honey of course, which isn't always listed as prominently as it should be, so be sure to read the label before purchasing.

- **Hands-On Time: 5 minutes**
- **Cook Time: 35 minutes**

Serves 4

2 tablespoons vegetable oil, divided

½ cup diced yellow onion

1 tablespoon wasabi powder

4 cups plus 1 tablespoon water

1 cup dried chickpeas

1 cup barbecue sauce

WASABI

Wasabi is a condiment also known as Japanese horseradish. It has a spicy and pungent flavor that is known to clear nasal passages if enough is consumed.

1 Press the Sauté button on the Instant Pot® and heat 1 tablespoon oil. Sauté the onions 4–5 minutes until translucent.

2 Reconstitute the wasabi powder by combining it with 1 tablespoon water, then add to the sautéed onions. Remove from the pot and set aside.

3 Add the chickpeas, remaining water, and 1 tablespoon oil to the pot and stir to combine thoroughly. Lock the lid into place, press the Bean button, and cook for default time of 30 minutes.

4 When the timer beeps, let the pressure release naturally for 10 minutes. Quick-release any remaining pressure until float valve drops and then unlock lid.

5 Add the onion mixture and barbecue sauce and stir to combine thoroughly.

Lentil Pâté

It's the fat that makes a pâté, and that's not always easy to find in vegetables. For other reliable vegan pâté options, try ground beans, mushrooms, or even mix in some avocado. Experiment with the cooking time on this dish: some cooks find the lentils take slightly less time to cook than the time provided here.

- **Hands-On Time: 5 minutes**
- **Cook Time: 35 minutes**

Serves 8

2 tablespoons olive oil, divided
1 cup diced yellow onion
3 cloves garlic, minced
1 teaspoon red wine vinegar
2 cups dried green lentils
4 cups water
1 teaspoon salt
Pinch freshly ground black pepper

SERVING SUGGESTIONS

For an eye-pleasing presentation, pour the pâté into a lightly oiled ramekin and pack tightly. Flip the ramekin over onto a serving dish and gently remove the pâté. Serve with a variety of crackers and baguette slices.

1 Press the Sauté button on the Instant Pot® and heat 1 tablespoon oil. Sauté the onions 2–3 minutes or until translucent. Add the garlic and vinegar, and sauté 30 more seconds.

2 Add the lentils, water, remaining oil, and salt to the pot and stir to combine thoroughly. Lock the lid into place, press the Bean button, and cook for default time of 30 minutes.

3 When the timer beeps, let pressure release naturally for 10 minutes. Quick-release any remaining pressure until float valve drops and then unlock lid.

4 Transfer lentil mixture to a food processor or blender and blend until smooth. Season with pepper and serve warm.

Baba Ghanoush

Often translated as "pampered daddy," baba ghanoush is a dish from the Middle East that's captured the world's imagination for centuries. At 12 minutes of cooking time, this dish is tailor-made for your Instant Pot®. Try it with toasted pita chips or as a vegetable dip.

- **Hands-On Time: 10 minutes**
- **Cook Time: 12 minutes**

Serves 4–6 (Yields 1½ cups)

1 tablespoon sesame oil

1 large eggplant, peeled and diced

4 cloves garlic, peeled and minced

½ cup water

3 tablespoons fresh Italian flat-leaf parsley

½ teaspoon salt

2 tablespoons fresh lemon juice

2 tablespoons tahini

1 tablespoon extra-virgin olive oil

1 Press the Sauté button on the Instant Pot® and add the sesame oil. Add the eggplant and sauté until it begins to soften, about 5 minutes. Add the garlic and sauté 30 seconds.

2 Add the water and lock the lid into place. Press the Manual button and adjust the timer to 6 minutes. When the timer beeps, quick-release pressure until float valve drops and then unlock lid.

3 Strain the cooked eggplant and garlic and add to a food processor or blender along with the parsley, salt, lemon juice, and tahini. Pulse to process. Scrape down the sides of the food processor or blender if necessary.

4 Add the olive oil and process until smooth.

Stuffed Grape Leaves

A medium, 5-ounce lemon yields about 2 teaspoons of lemon zest and 2–3 tablespoons of lemon juice. For this recipe, make sure to start with at least a dozen lemons if you're squeezing the juice yourself.

- **Hands-On Time: 15 minutes**
- **Cook Time: 22 minutes**

Serves 16

⅓ cup olive oil

4 green onions, chopped

⅓ cup minced fresh mint

⅓ cup minced fresh Italian flat-leaf parsley

3 cloves garlic, minced

1 cup long-grain white rice

2 cups vegetable broth

1 teaspoon salt

¼ teaspoon freshly ground black pepper

½ teaspoon lemon zest

1 (16-ounce) jar grape leaves

2 cups water

½ cup fresh lemon juice

DOLMADES

Stuffed grape leaves are often referred to as dolmades, or just dolma (which means "stuffed" in Greek). Some versions call for spiced ground lamb or other ground meat to be added to the filling, but you can make them vegan with a rice and herb filling.

1 Press the Sauté button on the Instant Pot® and add the oil, green onions, mint, and parsley; sauté 2 minutes or until the scallions are soft. Add the garlic and sauté an additional 30 seconds. Add the rice and stir-fry 1 minute. Add the broth, salt, pepper, and lemon zest; stir to mix. Lock the lid into place, press the Manual button, and adjust timer to 8 minutes.

2 When the timer beeps, quick-release pressure until float valve drops and unlock lid. Transfer the rice mixture to a medium bowl.

3 Drain the grape leaves. Rinse them thoroughly in warm water and then arrange them rib side up on a work surface. Trim away any thick ribs. Spoon about 2 teaspoons rice mixture on each grape leaf; fold the sides of each leaf over the filling and then roll it from the bottom to the top. Repeat with each leaf. Arrange the stuffed leaves (seam-side down) in a single layer on the steam basket insert.

4 Pour the water into the Instant Pot®. Set the steam basket insert into the pot and pour the lemon juice over the stuffed grape leaves. Lock the lid into place. Press the Steam button and cook for the default time of 10 minutes.

5 When the timer beeps, quick-release pressure until float valve drops and unlock lid. Lift the steamer basket out of the pot and let the stuffed leaves rest 5 minutes. Serve hot or cold.

Black Bean Dip

Most bean dishes call for many hours of soaking before you can even begin cooking the beans. The Bean setting on your Instant Pot® takes care of that in a fraction of the time. To give this dip a little kick, you can substitute canned or bottled jalapeño pepper slices for the mild green chilies or add 2 teaspoons of chipotle powder.

- **Hands-On Time: 5 minutes**
- **Cook Time: 35 minutes**

Serves 12

1 tablespoon olive oil
1 small yellow onion, peeled and diced
3 cloves garlic, minced
1 cup dried black beans
2 cups water
1 (14.5-ounce) can diced tomatoes
2 (4-ounce) cans mild green chilies, finely chopped
1 teaspoon chili powder
½ teaspoon dried oregano
¼ cup finely chopped fresh cilantro
1 cup shredded vegan Monterey jack cheese
Pinch salt (optional)

1 Press the Sauté button on the Instant Pot® and add the oil. Add the onions and sauté 3 minutes or until soft. Add the garlic and sauté 30 seconds. Transfer onions and garlic to a small bowl and set aside.

2 Press the Bean button on the Instant Pot® and add the beans, water, tomatoes, chilies, chili powder, and oregano; stir well. Lock the lid into place and cook for the default time of 30 minutes.

3 When the timer beeps, quick-release pressure until float valve drops and then unlock lid. Transfer the mixture to a food processor or blender. Add the onion and garlic mixture and cilantro and cheese and process until smooth. Taste for seasoning and add salt if desired.

4 Transfer dip to a serving bowl. Serve warm.

OTHER BEAN OPTIONS
Bean dips are delicious when made with a variety of dried beans. To complement the flavors in this recipe, use black beans, pinto beans, or white beans. If you're pressed for time, use canned beans instead of dried beans, but be sure to drain the liquid first.

Steamed Spring Rolls

Serve with a spicy peanut sauce or a sweet-and-sour dipping sauce to bring out the traditional Southeast Asian essence of these rolls. You'll rarely find a fresher, straight-from-the-garden quality to spring rolls than in this easy Instant Pot® dish.

- **Hands-On Time: 10 minutes**
- **Cook Time: 5 minutes**

Serves 12

1 cup shredded napa cabbage

1 cup sliced bamboo shoots

¼ cup chopped fresh cilantro

2 cloves garlic, minced

5 shiitake mushrooms, sliced

2 medium carrots, peeled and grated

1 teaspoon soy sauce

1 teaspoon rice wine vinegar

12 spring roll wrappers

2 cups water

SPRING ROLL WRAPPERS

Spring roll wrappers are also known as rice paper because they are made from rice flour, and rolled into thin, translucent sheets. Before using them you must briefly soak them in water so they become soft and pliable for rolling up the spring roll filling.

1 Combine the cabbage, bamboo shoots, cilantro, garlic, mushrooms, carrots, soy sauce, and vinegar in a medium bowl. Stir until just combined.

2 Place the spring roll wrappers on a flat surface.

3 Top each wrapper with an equal amount of the cabbage mixture, making a row down the center. Roll up the wrappers, tuck in the ends, and place side by side in the steamer basket.

4 Add the water to the Instant Pot® and insert the steamer basket. Lock the lid into place, press the Steam button, and adjust cook time to 3 minutes. When the timer beeps, let pressure release naturally until float valve drops and then unlock lid. Remove rolls from pot and serve warm.

Hummus

Hummus, an ancient dish made with chickpeas and sesame seeds, can be enhanced with a variety of flavors. While hummus can be thrown together quite quickly in a food processor, the real contribution of the Instant Pot® here is to allow you to bring this dish together using dried beans instead of canned in just 30 minutes. Add roasted red peppers, roasted garlic, or sun-dried tomatoes to spice up this basic recipe.

- **Hands-On Time: 5 minutes**
- **Cook Time: 30 minutes**

Yields 2 cups

1 cup dried chickpeas
4 cups water
¼ cup plus 1 tablespoon
    extra-virgin olive oil
2 teaspoons ground cumin
¾ teaspoon freshly ground
    black pepper
¾ teaspoon salt
⅓ cup fresh lemon juice
1 teaspoon minced garlic
⅓ cup tahini

1 Press the Bean button on the Instant Pot® and add the chickpeas, 4 cups water, and 1 tablespoon oil. Lock the lid into place and cook the beans for the default time of 30 minutes.

2 When the timer beeps, quick-release pressure until float valve drops and then unlock lid. Drain, carefully reserving the cooking liquid.

3 Place all remaining ingredients, including the cooked chickpeas, in a food processor and blend until creamy. If the consistency is too thick, add some of the reserved cooking liquid a little at a time until the hummus reaches your desired consistency. Serve chilled or at room temperature alongside chips or prepared vegetables for dipping. The mixture can be stored in an airtight container in the fridge 1–2 days.

4

Sauces, Jams, and Chutneys

On busy nights it's all too easy to open a can or jar for the sauce you need. With an Instant Pot® you can have flavorful sauces in minutes while your main dish is being prepared—all without the artificial or questionable ingredients in store-bought products. From Vodka Sauce and Roasted Red Pepper Sauce to White Bean Alfredo Sauce, this chapter will help you create amazing sauces that will complement any meal.

Additionally you'll find recipes for chutneys, relishes, jellies, and jams that will lighten up any meal and give your dishes that extra zing they need. You'll be able to create Caribbean Relish, Green Tomato Chutney, Blueberry Jam, and Easy Grape Jelly—all cooked in a fraction of the time!

Espagnole

In the early twentieth century, the now-legendary chef Auguste Escoffier formalized recipes for what he called the five "mother sauces" at the root of French cooking. One such sauce, Espagnole, which begins with a dark brown roux, provides the foundation for sauces such as bourguignonne, aux champignons, demi-glace, and countless others. Escoffier and his contemporaries lingered at their stovetops for hours preparing their espagnoles; you can plan to linger at your Instant Pot® for only about 20 minutes.

- **Hands-On Time: 10 minutes**
- **Cook Time: 10-13 minutes**

Yields 3 cups

¼ cup vegan margarine

1 small carrot, peeled and chopped

1 medium white onion, peeled and chopped

¼ cup all-purpose flour

4 cups vegetable broth, warmed

¼ cup canned tomato purée

2 large cloves garlic, chopped

1 medium stalk celery, chopped

½ teaspoon whole black peppercorns

1 bay leaf

WHAT IS A ROUX?

A roux is a blend of equal parts fat—such as butter, margarine, or oil—and flour that is used to thicken sauces. It's cooked over various levels of heat and different lengths of time to achieve either a white, blond, or brown roux.

1. Press the Sauté button on the Instant Pot®. Melt the margarine and sauté the carrot and onion about 2 minutes until the onion is golden brown. Add the flour and whisk to form a roux. Continue to cook, stirring continuously, until the roux is thickened and medium brown, about 1 minute. Add the hot broth, whisking vigorously throughout to prevent lumps.

2. Add the tomato purée, garlic, celery, peppercorns, and bay leaf to the pot. Lock the lid into place, press the Manual button on the pot, and adjust timer to 5 minutes. When the timer beeps, let pressure release naturally until float valve drops and then unlock lid.

3. Press the Sauté button on the pot and bring the sauce to a simmer; cook, uncovered, until reduced to 3 cups, stirring frequently.

4. Remove and discard the solids from the sauce with a slotted ladling spoon before serving. Store remaining mixture in an airtight container with a tight-fitting lid in the refrigerator up to 5–7 days.

Béchamel Sauce

Béchamel is another of France's "mother sauces," a rich creamy white sauce that developed in Italy and is the foundation of Alfredo sauce. The vegan preparation shared here is tasty and surprisingly light compared to traditional versions. Make sure the soy milk you choose is the unsweetened kind, not the more common vanilla or even "original" version.

- **Hands-On Time: 5 minutes**
- **Cook Time: 10-12 minutes**

Yields 3 cups

½ cup vegan margarine
½ cup all-purpose flour
4 cups unsweetened soy milk, warmed
1 teaspoon salt
1 teaspoon freshly ground black pepper

1 Press the Sauté button on the Instant Pot® and melt the margarine. Add the flour and stir 1–2 minutes to create a roux.

2 Gradually add the warmed milk to the pot, whisking until there are no lumps. Lock the lid into place, press the Manual button, and adjust timer to 7 minutes. When the timer beeps, let pressure release naturally until float valve drops and then unlock lid.

3 Season with salt and pepper. Store any remaining mixture in an airtight container with a tight-fitting lid in the refrigerator up to 2 days.

Au Jus

Look for a good faux beef broth for this dish. Vegetable broth is acceptable, but your jus won't have quite the same light gravy flavor that makes this sauce a staple. Red wine adds a lot of flavor, but if you don't want to add alcohol, a bit of vinegar is a good substitute.

- **Hands-On Time: 10 minutes**
- **Cook Time: 20 minutes**

Yields 1½ cups

1 tablespoon vegan margarine

1 shallot, peeled and minced

1 tablespoon all-purpose flour

2 cups faux beef broth or vegetable broth

1 cup dry red wine

¼ teaspoon liquid smoke

1 teaspoon salt

1 teaspoon freshly ground black pepper

1 Press the Sauté button on the Instant Pot® and add the margarine. Sauté the shallots until golden brown, about 2–3 minutes. Stir in the flour 1–2 minutes to create a roux.

2 Add the broth, red wine, liquid smoke, salt, and pepper to the pot and whisk until blended. Lock the lid into place, press the Manual button, and adjust timer to 7 minutes. When the timer beeps, let pressure release naturally until float valve drops and then unlock lid.

3 Press the Sauté button on the pot, and continue to simmer the au jus over low heat until reduced by half, about 5–7 minutes.

COOKING WITH WINE

Many people think that when you cook with wine you can use a lower quality product than you would if you were drinking it. However, as a general rule, if you wouldn't drink it, you shouldn't cook with it. The flavors will still come through, even cooked.

Beurre Blanc

This simple Beurre Blanc—it translates literally as "white butter"—will support most anything you could think to add—try your favorite herbs, spices, or even fruit! Although vinegar is often a good substitute for wine in recipes, it isn't a good choice here. If you prefer not to use wine in this sauce, try Vegetable Broth or Mushroom Broth instead (see the recipes in Chapter 5), which will also add a bit of sweetness.

- **Hands-On Time: 5 minutes**
- **Cook Time: 10 minutes**

Yields 1 cup

2 cups dry white wine
1 tablespoon minced shallot
2 cups cold vegan margarine, cut into cubes
1 teaspoon salt

1 Press the Sauté button on the Instant Pot® and adjust setting to Low. Heat the wine and shallots and bring to a simmer. Let the wine reduce to half.

2 Whisk in the cubes of margarine gradually, adding a few at a time to create an emulsion.

3 Once all the margarine has been whisked into the sauce, lock the lid into place. Press the Manual button and adjust timer to 5 minutes. When the timer beeps, quick-release pressure until float valve drops and then unlock lid.

4 Season with salt and serve.

Garden Marinara Sauce

If you have your own vegetable garden, what better dish to show it off than this Garden Marinara Sauce? The portion of fennel is kept low here, to just ½ teaspoon, as it might be an unfamiliar flavor so some, especially in a savory dish. The already converted will probably want to add more.

- **Hands-On Time: 10 minutes**
- **Cook Time: 15 minutes**

Serves 4

2 tablespoons olive oil

1 large sweet onion, peeled and diced

1 small red bell pepper, seeded and diced

1 large carrot, peeled and grated

4 cloves garlic, minced

1 tablespoon dried parsley

½ teaspoon dried ground fennel

1 teaspoon dried basil

1 bay leaf

Pinch dried red pepper flakes

¼ teaspoon salt

1 (14.5-ounce) can diced tomatoes in sauce

½ cup vegetable broth

1 Press the Sauté button on the Instant Pot® and add the oil. Add the onion, bell pepper, and carrots, and sauté 3 minutes. Stir in the garlic and sauté an additional 30 seconds.

2 Stir the remaining ingredients into the pot. Lock the lid into place, press the Manual button, and adjust timer to 10 minutes. When the timer beeps, quick-release pressure until float valve drops and then unlock lid.

3 Stir the sauce and discard the bay leaf. If desired, use an immersion blender to purée the sauce in the pot. Store remaining mixture in an airtight container with a tight-fitting lid in the refrigerator up to 2–3 days, or the freezer up to 1 week.

Fresh Tomato Sauce

A simple tomato sauce recipe is a must for any kitchen, and your Instant Pot® makes this one a snap to prepare. You can use this sauce immediately, refrigerate it in a covered container up to 1 week, or freeze it up to 6 months.

- **Hands-On Time: 5 minutes**
- **Cook Time: 20 minutes**

Yields 4 cups

2 tablespoons olive oil

2 cloves garlic, minced

2½ pounds vine-ripened tomatoes, peeled and diced (retain their juice)

1 teaspoon dried parsley

1 teaspoon dried basil

1 tablespoon balsamic vinegar

½ teaspoon granulated sugar

Pinch salt

Pinch freshly ground black pepper

1 Press the Sauté button on the Instant Pot® and add the oil. Add the garlic and sauté 30 seconds.

2 Add the tomatoes to the pot along with their juice. Add the remaining ingredients to the pot and lock the lid into place. Press the Manual button and adjust timer to 10 minutes. When the timer beeps, let pressure release naturally until float valve drops and then unlock lid.

3 Stir the sauce. If you prefer a thicker sauce, press the Sauté button, adjust setting to Low, and simmer uncovered 10 minutes or until it reaches the desired thickness.

BALANCING THE ACIDITY

When tasting tomato sauce and thinking "what else do I need to add?" many cooks reach for additional salt, but that might not be the ingredient you need. To balance out the acidity—the taste you may be trying to omit— try adding sugar or even grated carrot to the sauce.

Simple Marinara Sauce

This bright, fresh sauce emerged centuries ago in Naples and has become that maritime city's most beloved export. It's also one of Instant Pot®'s opportunities to show off. Serve hot over pasta, rice, or vegetables. For a more savory marinara, add cooked Boca Veggie Ground Crumbles or any similar vegan meat substitute.

- **Hands-On Time: 5 minutes**
- **Cook Time: 12 minutes**

Serves 4

2 tablespoons olive oil

½ medium yellow onion, peeled and diced

2 cloves garlic, minced

2 (14.5-ounce) cans diced tomatoes

½ teaspoon granulated sugar

1 tablespoon tomato paste

⅓ cup water

1 tablespoon fresh lemon juice

2 tablespoons chopped fresh basil

Pinch salt

Pinch freshly ground black pepper

1 Press the Sauté button on the Instant Pot® and add the oil. Sauté the onion until golden brown, about 3–5 minutes. Add the garlic and sauté an additional 30 seconds.

2 Add the tomatoes, sugar, tomato paste, and water to the pot. Lock the lid into place, press the Manual button, and adjust timer to 6 minutes. When the timer beeps, let pressure release naturally until float valve drops and then unlock lid.

3 Stir in the lemon juice, basil, salt, and pepper. Store in an airtight container with a tight-fitting lid in the refrigerator 2–3 days, or in the freezer up to 1 week.

Vodka Sauce

Cooking with alcohol helps bring out flavors in some foods, including tomatoes, making Vodka Sauce one of the most popular tomato sauces in Italian-American cuisine. Note: it's commonly believed that alcohol cooks off quickly, leaving dishes like this one alcohol-free. That's not so. If anyone at your table is avoiding alcohol, it's best to pick a different sauce.

- **Hands-On Time: 5 minutes**
- **Cook Time: 22 minutes**

Serves 4

2 tablespoons olive oil

½ medium yellow onion, peeled and diced

2 cloves garlic, minced

1 teaspoon dried red pepper flakes

1 cup vodka

2 (14.5-ounce) cans diced tomatoes

2 tablespoons tomato paste

⅓ cup water

1 cup unsweetened soy milk or vegan cream

2 tablespoons chopped fresh Italian flat-leaf parsley

2 tablespoons chopped fresh basil

Pinch salt

Pinch freshly ground black pepper

1 Press the Sauté button on the Instant Pot® and add the olive oil. Sauté the onions until golden brown, about 3–5 minutes. Add the garlic and red pepper flakes, and sauté an additional minute. Add the vodka and simmer about 10 minutes.

2 Add the diced tomatoes, tomato paste, and water to the pot. Lock the lid into place, press the Manual button, and adjust timer to 5 minutes. When the timer beeps, let pressure release naturally until float valve drops and then unlock lid.

3 Press the Sauté button and adjust setting to low. Stir in the soy milk or cream and simmer 2 minutes. Add the parsley, basil, salt, and pepper. Store remaining mixture in an airtight container in the refrigerator 2–3 days or in the freezer up to 1 week.

Roasted Red Pepper Sauce

Instant Pot® can handle this sauce in under 10 minutes—assuming of course you save time by using canned or jarred roasted red peppers instead of roasting them yourself. Another option is to step back one move and sauté the peppers instead, right there in the Instant Pot®.

- **Hands-On Time: 5 minutes**
- **Cook Time: 7 minutes**

Serves 4

2 cups roasted red peppers
2 cups vegetable broth
2 tablespoons red wine vinegar
2 tablespoons extra-virgin olive oil
1 teaspoon garlic powder
½ cup fresh basil
Pinch salt
Pinch freshly ground black pepper

1 Add the red peppers, broth, vinegar, and oil to a food processor or blender and purée until smooth. Pour the mixture into the Instant Pot®.

2 Add the garlic powder to the pot and stir. Lock the lid into place, press the Manual button, and adjust timer to 7 minutes. When the timer beeps, let pressure release naturally until float valve drops and then unlock lid.

3 Add the basil, salt, and pepper before serving. Store remaining mixture in an airtight container with a tight-fitting lid up to 2–3 days in the refrigerator or 1 week in the freezer.

White Bean Alfredo Sauce

Using white beans as the base of a creamy sauce eliminates the dairy and reduces the fat in the recipe, making for a much healthier alternative. This preparation specifies cannellini beans, but navy, great northern, or baby lima beans can all be substituted.

- **Hands-On Time: 5 minutes**
- **Cook Time: 27 minutes**

Serves 4

¼ cup vegan margarine
2 cloves garlic, minced
1 cup dried cannellini beans
4 cups water
1 cup unsweetened soy milk
1 teaspoon fresh lemon juice
1½ teaspoons salt
½ teaspoon freshly ground
  black pepper

FLAVOR VARIATIONS
This recipe is for a basic sauce. Feel free to add ingredients of your choice. Try sprinkling in a blend of earthy herbs, such as thyme, sage, and oregano, or diced fresh tomatoes.

1   Press the Sauté button on the Instant Pot® and add the margarine. Sauté the garlic 2 minutes, stirring continuously.

2   Add the beans and water to the pot. Lock the lid into place, press the Bean button, and adjust time to 25 minutes. When the timer beeps, quick-release pressure until float valve drops and then unlock lid.

3   Pour the beans into a blender or food processor in batches and purée. The mixture will be thick.

4   Press the Sauté button on the pot, adjust setting to Low, and slowly stir in the soy milk until desired consistency is reached. Add lemon juice, salt, and pepper, and heat until warm.

Spicy Peanut Sauce

Americans generally eat a Spicy Peanut Sauce with Thai recipes—spring or summer rolls, Thai noodle dishes, and so on—but we shouldn't restrict it to just those dishes. Consider all the foods with which peanuts pair and get creative. One place to start: celery sticks and carrots.

- **Hands-On Time: 5 minutes**
- **Cook Time: 5 minutes**

Yields 1½ cups

½ cup smooth peanut butter

2 tablespoons maple syrup

2 cloves garlic

1" piece ginger, peeled and chopped

¼ cup rice vinegar

¼ cup sesame oil

1 teaspoon cayenne pepper

1 teaspoon ground cumin

2 teaspoons dried red pepper flakes

1 cup water

Pinch salt

Pinch freshly ground black pepper

1 In a blender or food processor, combine all ingredients except salt and pepper, adding the water a little at a time to achieve desired consistency.

2 Pour the mixture into the Instant Pot® and lock the lid into place. Press the Manual button and adjust timer to 5 minutes. When the timer beeps, let pressure release naturally until float valve drops and then unlock lid.

3 Add salt and pepper before serving. Store remaining mixture in an airtight container with a tight-fitting lid in the refrigerator up to 2–3 days, or in the freezer up to 1 week.

Blueberry Jam

With its nutmeg and orange zest, this is a more complex jam than the Strawberry Jam featured in this chapter, but you won't notice much of a difference in time or preparation. Note: a 6-ounce bottle of liquid pectin can be substituted for the dry pectin in this recipe.

- **Hands-On Time: 15 minutes**
- **Cook Time: 5 minutes**

Yields 4 cups

4 cups blueberries
4 cups granulated sugar
1 cup orange juice
1 teaspoon orange zest
Pinch freshly ground nutmeg
Pinch salt
1 (1.75-ounce) package dry
    pectin

1 Add the blueberries, sugar, orange juice, orange zest, nutmeg, and salt to the Instant Pot®. Stir to combine. Lock the lid into place, press the Manual button, and adjust timer to 4 minutes. When the timer beeps, let pressure release naturally until float valve drops and then unlock lid.

2 Push the blueberry mixture through a strainer and return the pulp to the Instant Pot®. Press the Sauté button on the pot and adjust setting to High. Stir in the pectin, and bring the mixture to a rolling boil, stirring constantly. Continue to boil and stir for 1 minute.

3 Skim off and discard any foam. Ladle into hot, sterilized glass containers or jars, leaving 1" headspace. Seal the containers or jars. (If you prefer, you can follow the instructions that came with your canning jars and process the preserves for shelf storage.)

4 Let cool and serve. Store remaining mixture in the refrigerator up to 1 week or in the freezer up to 1 month.

Country Barbecue Sauce

You can offer this barbecue sauce as a dipping sauce or use it for grilling as a wet-mop sauce. Whatever you choose, remember to check the label on your Worcestershire sauce before purchasing, as some varieties do contain fish.

- **Hands-On Time: 5 minutes**
- **Cook Time: 10 minutes**

Yields 5 cups

4 cups ketchup

½ cup apple cider vinegar

½ cup vegetarian Worcestershire sauce

½ cup firmly packed light brown sugar

¼ cup molasses

¼ cup prepared yellow mustard

2 tablespoons barbecue seasoning mix

1 teaspoon freshly ground black pepper

1 tablespoon liquid smoke, or to taste (optional)

2 tablespoons hot sauce, or to taste (optional)

Pinch salt, or to taste (optional)

1   Add all ingredients except optional seasonings to the Instant Pot® and stir to combine. Lock the lid into place, press the Manual button, and adjust timer to 10 minutes. When the timer beeps, quick-release pressure until float valve drops and then unlock lid.

2   Taste for seasoning and add the optional seasonings to taste if desired. Ladle into sterilized glass jars. Cover and store in the refrigerator up to 3 months.

BARBECUE SEASONING

Barbecue seasoning is a blend of herbs and spices that can be found in the spice aisle of your local grocery store. To make your own, mix equal parts of brown sugar, ground red pepper, salt, garlic powder, onion powder, paprika, and dried oregano.

Plum Sauce

The sweet-and-sour flavors of this sauce trace their roots to Chinese cooking. Plum Sauce is often served with egg rolls, but you can also use it as a glaze on tofu or vegetables. If plums are out of season or just not to your liking, you can substitute oranges, peaches, and other similar fruit.

- **Hands-On Time: 10 minutes**
- **Cook Time: 12 minutes**

Yields 4 cups

8 cups (about 3 pounds) plums, pitted and cut in half

1 small sweet onion, peeled and diced

1 cup water

1 teaspoon minced fresh ginger

1 clove garlic, minced

¾ cup granulated sugar

½ cup rice vinegar or apple cider vinegar

1 teaspoon ground coriander

½ teaspoon salt

½ teaspoon ground cinnamon

¼ teaspoon cayenne pepper

¼ teaspoon ground cloves

1 Add the plums, onion, water, ginger, and garlic to the Instant Pot®. Lock the lid into place, press the Manual button, and adjust timer to 7 minutes. When the timer beeps, quick-release pressure until float valve drops and then unlock lid.

2 Use an immersion blender to thoroughly blend and combine the mixture before straining, or press the cooked plum mixture through a sieve to complete.

3 Return the mixture to the pot and stir in the sugar, vinegar, coriander, salt, cinnamon, cayenne, and cloves. Lock the lid into place, press the Manual button, and adjust timer to 5 minutes. When the timer beeps, quick-release pressure until float valve drops and then unlock lid. Check the sauce; it should have the consistency of applesauce. If it isn't thick enough, press the Sauté button on the pot and simmer until desired consistency is achieved.

Cranberry-Apple Chutney

Chutney, an Indian staple that has traveled most of the world, is often made in huge quantities because of the traditional preparation time. The Instant Pot® can help you make plenty for the neighbors and in-laws, or you can just make this quick batch and be on your way.

- **Hands-On Time: 5 minutes**
- **Cook Time: 15 minutes**

Serves 16

1 (12-ounce) bag cranberries
1 cup packed light brown sugar
1 small sweet onion, peeled and diced
1 jalapeño pepper, seeded and minced
2 tablespoons grated fresh ginger
1 clove garlic, minced
1 teaspoon yellow mustard seed
1 (3") cinnamon stick
1 teaspoon fresh lemon juice
¼ teaspoon salt
3 pounds tart cooking apples
Ground ginger, to taste (optional)
Ground cinnamon, to taste (optional)

1 Press the Sauté button on the Instant Pot®. Add the cranberries, brown sugar, onion, jalapeño, ginger, garlic, mustard, cinnamon, lemon juice, and salt to the pot; cook until the sugar dissolves, about 10–12 minutes, stirring occasionally.

2 Peel and core the apples; cut into 1" strips. Place the apples in a layer over the cranberry mixture in the pot. Do not stir the apples into the mixture.

3 Lock the lid into place. Press the Steam button on the pot and adjust timer to 3 minutes. When the timer beeps, quick-release pressure until float valve drops and then unlock lid.

4 Remove the cinnamon stick. Taste for seasoning and add ginger and cinnamon if desired.

5 Store in a covered container in the refrigerator up to 2 weeks. Serve heated or chilled.

FOR BEST RESULTS
Placing the apples over the cranberry mixture prevents the cranberries from foaming as they cook. If you'd like to make cranberry-pear chutney, substitute 3 pounds of peeled and cored ripe Bartlett pears for the apples.

Green Tomato Chutney

If you prefer spicy chutney, you can substitute 1 Anaheim chili and either 4 small red chilies or 4 jalapeño peppers for the red bell peppers. Green tomatoes—not a variety but simply unripe red tomatoes—are generally available throughout the summer and fall.

- **Hands-On Time: 10 minutes**
- **Cook Time: 12 minutes**

Yields 5 cups

2 pounds green tomatoes, stemmed and diced

1 white onion, peeled, quartered lengthwise, and thinly sliced

2 medium red bell peppers, seeded and diced

¼ cup dried currants

2 tablespoons grated fresh ginger

¾ cup firmly packed dark brown sugar

¾ cup dry white wine

Pinch sea salt

1 Put all ingredients in the Instant Pot® and stir to combine. Lock the lid into place, press the Manual button, and adjust timer to 12 minutes. When the timer beeps, let pressure release naturally until float valve drops and then unlock lid.

2 Transfer the chutney to an airtight container and refrigerate overnight before serving. It can be stored in a covered container in the refrigerator 2 months.

Strawberry Jam

Nothing says sunlight and summertime quite like this simple, perfect Strawberry Jam. You can marinate the berries in the sugar right there in the Instant Pot®. If you don't have a potato masher handy for the fruit crushing and mixing, a blender is fine. Don't have one of those either? Time to get handy with a whisk!

- **Hands-On Time: 15 minutes**
- **Cook Time: 10 minutes**

Yields 4 cups

4 cups quartered
    strawberries
3 cups granulated sugar
¼ cup fresh lemon juice

1 Add the strawberries and sugar to the Instant Pot® and stir. Let marinate 1 hour or until the strawberries are juicy.

2 Use a potato masher to crush the fruit and mix in the sugar until the sugar is dissolved. Stir in the lemon juice.

3 Lock the lid into place, press the Manual button, and adjust timer to 7 minutes. When the timer beeps, let pressure release naturally until float valve drops and then unlock lid.

4 Press the Sauté button on the pot and adjust setting to High. Boil 3 minutes or until jam reaches the desired gel state.

5 Skim off and discard any foam. Ladle into hot, sterilized glass containers or jars, leaving ½" headspace. Seal the containers or jars. (If you prefer, you can follow the instructions that came with your canning jars and process the preserves for shelf storage.)

6 Let cool and serve. Store remaining mixture in an airtight container with a tight-fitting lid 2–3 days in the refrigerator, or 1 week in the freezer.

Dried Apricot Preserves

Never fill the Instant Pot® more than halfway when making preserves, chutneys, or other fruit dishes. Of course, you should never fill it more than two-thirds with liquids under any circumstances or your device won't be able to function properly. A conversion note on the cinnamon sticks: 1 3" stick is roughly equivalent to ½ teaspoon ground cinnamon. The taste drop-off is significant, and it's worth an extra trip to the grocer to find the sticks, but the preserves will pack plenty of flavor either way.

- **Hands-On Time: 15 minutes**
- **Cook Time: 15 minutes**

Yields 7 cups

4 cups chopped dried apricots

2 cups water

5 black peppercorns

5 cardamom pods

2 (3") cinnamon sticks

2 star anise

½ cup lemon juice

4 cups granulated sugar

DETERMINING THE GEL POINT
Test a small amount of preserves by spooning it onto an ice-cold plate. It has reached the gel point when it's as thick as you desire. A softer set is ideal for use in sauces; if you prefer a firm, jam-like consistency, you may need to continue to boil the mixture up to 20 minutes.

1   Add the apricots to a large bowl. Pour in the water, cover, and let the apricots soak 24 hours at room temperature.

2   Wrap the peppercorns, cardamom, cinnamon, and star anise in cheesecloth and secure with kitchen string.

3   Add the apricots, soaking water, lemon juice, and spice bag to the Instant Pot®. Lock the lid into place, press the Manual button, and adjust timer to 10 minutes. When the timer beeps, let pressure release naturally until float valve drops and then unlock lid.

4   Discard the cheesecloth spice bag and stir in the sugar. Press the Sauté button on the pot and adjust setting to High. Boil covered 4–5 minutes or until the apricot mixture reaches the gel point.

5   Skim off and discard any foam. Ladle into hot, sterilized glass containers or jars, leaving ½" headspace. Seal the containers or jars. (If you prefer, you can follow the instructions that came with your canning jars and process the preserves for shelf storage.)

6   Let cool and serve. Store remaining mixture in an airtight container with a tight-fitting lid in the refrigerator 2–3 days or the freezer up to 1 week.

Caribbean Relish

Think of this relish as a Caribbean spin on hummus. It's not really, of course, but the tahini provides a familiar taste to this exciting relish for those unfamiliar with Caribbean flavors. The mingling of the tahini, pineapple, and beans is the heart of this memorable condiment.

- **Hands-On Time: 5 minutes**
- **Cook Time: 30 minutes**

Serves 12

1½ cups red or white kidney beans

7 cups water

2 teaspoons vegetable oil

Pinch salt

2 tablespoons tahini paste

¾ cup crushed pineapple, drained

4 cloves garlic, minced

¼ teaspoon ground cumin

¼ teaspoon ground ginger

¼ teaspoon freshly ground white pepper

½ cup minced fresh cilantro

1   Add the beans, water, and oil to the Instant Pot®. Lock the lid into place, press the Bean button, and cook for the default time of 30 minutes. When the timer beeps, let pressure release naturally until float valve drops and then unlock lid. Drain beans.

2   Add the cooked beans to a blender or food processor along with all the remaining ingredients. Pulse until mixed but still chunky. Transfer to a covered container and chill until ready to serve.

TOMATO RELISH

To make a tasty tomato relish: Peel, seed, and dice 2 large tomatoes. Add to a medium bowl and mix them together with ½ cup thawed frozen corn kernels, ¼ cup extra-virgin olive oil, and 6 diced scallions. Season with salt, freshly ground black pepper, and fresh lime juice to taste.

Blackberry Jam

Blackberries are great as they are in season seemingly all summer in most of the US, but you have plenty of options here; experiment with other berries, or try a combination of a few. This may be the perfect complement to your favorite vegan frozen treat!

- **Hands-On Time: 15 minutes**
- **Cook Time: 10 minutes**

Yields 4 cups

4 cups blackberries
4 cups granulated sugar
1 cup orange juice
1 teaspoon fresh lemon juice
Pinch salt
1 (1.75-ounce) package dry
    pectin

1 Add the blackberries, sugar, orange juice, lemon juice, and salt to the Instant Pot® and stir to combine. Lock the lid into place, press the Manual button, and adjust timer to 5 minutes. When the timer beeps, let pressure release naturally until float valve drops and then unlock lid.

2 Push the blackberry mixture through a strainer and return the pulp to the pot. Press the Sauté button and adjust setting to High. Stir in the pectin and bring mixture to a rolling boil, stirring constantly. Continue to boil and stir 1 minute.

3 Skim off and discard any foam. Ladle into hot, sterilized glass containers or jars, leaving 1" headspace. Seal the containers or jars. (If you prefer, you can follow the instructions that came with your canning jars and process the preserves for shelf storage.)

4 Let cool at room temperature 24 hours before canning. Refrigerate up to 5 weeks or freeze up to 8 months.

Peach Jam

Fresh, in-season fruit is the place to start for mouthwatering jams and jellies. The peach harvest runs from late summer through early autumn everywhere in the US but Florida, which brings in its peaches in May. Four cups is a lot of sugar, of course, but try this jam and then decide how much to worry about it.

- **Hands-On Time: 15 minutes**
- **Cook Time: 10 minutes**

Yields 4 cups

4 cups peeled and chopped peaches
4 cups granulated sugar
1 teaspoon fresh lemon juice
1 (1.75-ounce) package dry pectin

1 Add the peaches, sugar, and lemon juice to the Instant Pot®. Stir to combine. Lock the lid into place, press the Manual button, and adjust timer to 3 minutes. When the timer beeps, let pressure release naturally until float valve drops and then unlock lid.

2 Press the Sauté button on the pot and adjust setting to High. Stir in the pectin, and bring mixture to a rolling boil, stirring constantly. Continue to boil and stir 1 minute.

3 Skim off and discard any foam. Ladle into hot, sterilized glass containers or jars, leaving 1" headspace. Seal the containers or jars. (If you prefer, you can follow the instructions that came with your canning jars and process the preserves for shelf storage.)

4 Let cool at room temperature 24 hours before canning. Refrigerate up to 5 weeks or freeze up to 8 months.

Easy Grape Jelly

As far as we're concerned, this lunchbox staple is reborn a gourmet extravaganza when you make the jelly yourself. And we won't tell anyone that it took you less than 10 minutes with your Instant Pot®. We can't emphasize enough that you should use natural, whole juices, not diet or light ones. The latter can't be counted on to produce good jelly.

- **Hands-On Time: 5 minutes**
- **Cook Time: 3 minutes**

Yields 5 cups

5 cups grape juice
2 (1.75-ounce) package dry pectin
½ cup granulated sugar

1 Press the Sauté button on the Instant Pot® and adjust setting to Low. Add grape juice and pectin to the pot and stir to combine. Lock the lid into place, press the Manual button, and adjust timer to 3 minutes. When the timer beeps, quick-release pressure until float valve drops and then unlock lid.

2 Slowly stir in the sugar. Skim off and discard any foam. Ladle into hot, sterilized glass containers or jars, leaving 1" headspace. Seal the containers or jars. (If you prefer, you can follow the instructions that came with your canning jars and process the preserves for shelf storage.)

3 Let cool at room temperature 24 hours before canning. Refrigerate up to 5 weeks or freeze up to 8 months.

Soups, Chilis, and Stews

Sometimes you may have all the ingredients for a great soup, but you look at the clock and realize you are only an hour out from dinner. Typically you need low heat and a long cooking time to marry together all the wonderful spices and flavors that make any soup great, but not anymore. The pressurized heat in your Instant Pot® can save the day. Although there is a Slow Cook button on your Instant Pot® for when time isn't an issue, cooking at high pressure can have you serving a finished dinner within an hour. To cut back on time even more, you can find precut onions and peppers in the freezer section of your local grocery store that work great in a pinch.

Mushroom Broth

Make a big batch of this versatile base broth, which you may find yourself using in more dishes than you'd imagine and enjoying before it even makes it into the freezer. Fresh broth can be covered and refrigerated for 2 or 3 days, or it can be frozen for as long as 3 months.

- **Hands-On Time: 10 minutes**
- **Cook Time: 20 minutes**

Yields 8 cups

4 medium carrots, peeled and cut into large pieces

2 large leeks, trimmed and cut into large pieces

2 large yellow onions, peeled and quartered

1 large stalk celery, chopped

5 whole cloves

Pinch dried red pepper flakes

2 cups sliced button mushrooms

8½ cups water

1 Put all ingredients in the Instant Pot®. Lock the lid into place. Press the Soup button and adjust timer to 20 minutes. When the timer beeps, let pressure release naturally until float valve drops and then unlock lid.

2 Strain the broth through a fine-mesh strainer or through cheesecloth placed in a colander. Store in a covered container in the refrigerator or freezer.

Vegetable Broth

There is almost no end to the dishes that are enhanced by this hearty, homemade Vegetable Broth, many of which are included in this very book.

- **Hands-On Time: 5 minutes**
- **Cook Time: 30 minutes**

Yields 4 cups

2 large yellow onions, peeled and halved

2 medium carrots, peeled and cut into large pieces

3 large stalks celery, cut in half

1 head garlic, cloves separated and peeled

10 whole peppercorns

1 bay leaf

6 cups water

1　Add all the ingredients to the Instant Pot®. Lock the lid into place. Press the Soup button and cook for the default time of 30 minutes. When the timer beeps, let pressure release naturally until float valve drops and then remove lid.

2　Strain the stock through a fine-mesh strainer or through cheesecloth placed in a colander. Store in an airtight container in the refrigerator 2–3 days, or freeze up to 3 months.

Fresh Tomato Soup

This soup celebrates the wondrously simple taste of fresh vine-ripened tomatoes. You can add sautéed onion or shallots and herbs if you like, or let it stand on its own. Either way, it'll be ready in about 20 minutes. A true Instant Pot® standout.

- **Hands-On Time: 5 minutes**
- **Cook Time: 15 minutes**

Serves 4

8 medium fresh tomatoes, peeled, seeded, and diced (retain juice)

¼ teaspoon sea salt

1 cup water

½ teaspoon baking soda

2 cups unsweetened soy milk

Pinch freshly ground black pepper

1　Add the tomatoes along with any juice you can retain to the Instant Pot®. Stir in the salt and water. Press the Manual button on the pot and adjust timer to 5 minutes. When the timer beeps, quick-release pressure until float valve drops and then unlock lid.

2　Stir the baking soda into the tomato mixture. Once the soup has stopped bubbling and foaming, stir in the soy milk. Press the Sauté button on the pot and adjust setting to Low. Cook and stir for several minutes or until heated through. Add pepper and serve.

Minestrone

This Instant Pot® Minestrone bursts with vitality and nutrients. It is a great first course served before a salad or other light entrée, and it is also more than substantial enough to stand on its own. Depending on your knife skills you may find your prep time less or more than what is listed, but this simple classic Italian soup is worth your effort.

- **Hands-On Time: 10 minutes**
- **Cook Time: 16 minutes**

Serves 6

2 tablespoons olive oil

1 large yellow onion, peeled and diced

2 cloves garlic, minced

2 large carrots, peeled and diced

2 leeks, white part only, trimmed and diced

½ head green cabbage, cored and roughly chopped

2 medium stalks celery, diced

2 (14.5-ounce) cans diced tomatoes

¼ teaspoon dried rosemary

1 teaspoon dried parsley

¼ teaspoon dried oregano

4½ cups vegetable broth

½ cup dried elbow macaroni

½ cup Arborio rice

Pinch salt

Pinch freshly ground black pepper

1 Add the olive oil to the Instant Pot® and press the Sauté button. Add the onion and sauté 3 minutes or until soft. Stir in the garlic, carrots, leeks, cabbage, celery, undrained tomatoes, rosemary, parsley, oregano, and vegetable broth.

2 Lock the lid into place, press the Manual button, and adjust timer to 6 minutes. When the timer beeps, quick-release pressure until float valve drops and then unlock lid.

3 Stir in the macaroni and rice. Press the Manual button on the pot and adjust timer to 7 minutes. When the timer beeps, let pressure release naturally until float valve drops and then unlock lid.

4 Taste for seasoning and add salt, pepper, and additional herbs if desired.

Italian Pasta and Bean Soup

Experiment with the types of grains and beans in this soup. Smaller pastas or even couscous work well in this soup, which takes a bit longer to pull together than some Instant Pot® recipes, but yields a lavish soup because of the many delicious ingredients.

- **Hands-On Time: 10 minutes**
- **Cook Time: 30 minutes**

Serves 10

1 tablespoon extra-virgin olive oil

4 medium carrots, peeled and diced

2 medium stalks celery, diced

2 medium yellow onions, peeled and diced

3 cloves garlic, minced

1 teaspoon dried basil

1 teaspoon dried oregano

6 cups water

1 pound dried cannellini beans

1 bay leaf

1 teaspoon dried parsley

4 cups vegetable or mushroom broth

1½ cups elbow macaroni or small shell pasta

Pinch salt

Pinch freshly ground black pepper

1 Press the Sauté button on the Instant Pot® and add the oil. Add the carrots and celery; sauté 3 minutes. Add the onion and sauté 3 minutes or until the vegetables are soft. Add the garlic, basil, and oregano; sauté 30 seconds.

2 Add the water, beans, and bay leaf. Lock the lid into place. Press the Manual button and adjust time to 10 minutes. When the timer beeps, let pressure release naturally until float valve drops and then remove lid.

3 Discard the bay leaf. Add the parsley and broth to the pot. Lock the lid into place, press the Manual button, and adjust timer to 6 minutes. When the timer beeps, quick-release pressure until float valve drops and then remove lid.

4 Press the Sauté button on the pot and adjust setting to High. Stir in the pasta. Cook pasta al dente according to package directions, about 7 minutes. Season with salt and pepper. Serve warm.

Creamy White Bean and Garlic Soup

White bean purée is a great dairy alternative for achieving a creamy texture in soups. No particular need to insist on great northern beans in this dish—it's a popular variety, but any of the four major white beans will do just fine here.

- **Hands-On Time: 5 minutes**
- **Cook Time: 11 minutes**

Serves 8

3 tablespoons olive oil

1 medium yellow onion, peeled and sliced

6 cloves garlic, minced

6 cups vegetable broth

2 cups dried great northern beans

1 bay leaf

1 tablespoon chopped fresh rosemary

1 teaspoon fresh lemon juice

Pinch salt

Pinch freshly ground black pepper

1 Press the Sauté button on the Instant Pot® and add the oil. Add the onion and sauté until golden brown. Add the garlic and sauté about 1 minute.

2 Add the broth, beans, bay leaf, and rosemary to the pot. Lock the lid into place, press the Manual button, and adjust timer to 10 minutes. When the timer beeps, let pressure release naturally until float valve drops and then unlock lid.

3 Remove the bay leaf. Purée the soup in a food processor or blender. Add the lemon juice. Taste for seasoning and add salt and pepper.

Mushroom-Barley Soup

Umami—some call it a fifth flavor, some say it translates from Japanese more or less as "savory." Either way, the portobello cap lends an element of it to this traditional savory soup. If you can't locate pearl barley, use whatever you have on hand.

- **Hands-On Time: 10 minutes**
- **Cook Time: 30 minutes**

Serves 6

2 tablespoons vegan margarine

1 tablespoon olive or vegetable oil

2 medium stalks celery, diced

1 large carrot, peeled and diced

1 large sweet onion, peeled and sliced

2 cloves garlic, minced

1 portobello mushroom cap, diced

8 ounces button mushrooms, sliced

1 bay leaf

½ cup pearl barley

6 cups water

2 tablespoons vermouth or brandy (optional)

Pinch salt

Pinch freshly ground black pepper

1 Press the Sauté button on the Instant Pot® and melt the margarine with the oil. Add the celery and carrot and sauté 2 minutes. Add the onion and sauté 3 minutes or until the onion is translucent. Stir in the garlic and mushrooms; sauté 5 minutes or until the mushrooms release their moisture and the onion begins to turn golden.

2 Stir the bay leaf, barley, water, and vermouth or brandy (if using) into the pot. Lock the lid into place, press the Manual button, and adjust timer to 20 minutes. When the timer beeps, let pressure release naturally until float valve drops and then unlock lid.

3 Discard the bay leaf. Add salt and pepper. Serve warm.

PEARL BARLEY

Pearl barley is the type of barley that has the outer hull and the bran layer removed. It is one of the most commonly used varieties, but it isn't the most nutritious.

Lentil Soup

Lentils aren't beans, but along with peas they are part of the legume family to which beans belong. The big but apparently little-publicized difference: they don't have to soak before cooking. Lentils come in red, yellow, brown, and green, any of which will work in this amazingly quick Lentil Soup.

- **Hands-On Time: 5 minutes**
- **Cook Time: 13 minutes**

Serves 4

1 tablespoon olive oil

1 medium yellow onion, peeled and sliced

4 cloves garlic, minced

1 medium carrot, peeled and sliced

5 plum tomatoes, chopped

2 teaspoons dried tarragon

1 teaspoon dried thyme

1 teaspoon paprika

6 cups vegetable broth

2 cups lentils (color of choice)

2 bay leaves

Pinch salt

Pinch freshly ground black pepper

1 Press the Sauté button on the Instant Pot® and add the oil. Add the onions and sauté until they begin to turn golden. Add the garlic and carrots and continue sautéing 2–3 minutes.

2 Add the remaining ingredients except salt and pepper to the pot and stir to mix. Lock the lid into place, press the Manual button, and adjust timer to 10 minutes. When the timer beeps, let pressure release naturally until float valve drops and then unlock lid.

3 Remove the bay leaves and season with salt and pepper.

French Onion Soup

This recipe calls for vegetable or mushroom broth and red wine, which is a tasty substitute for the beef broth typically found in this soup. Another well-known feature of French Onion Soup is obviously the cheese, but you can't go wrong here if you use a quality vegan cheese. I recommend Daiya Mozzarella Style Shreds for this recipe.

- **Hands-On Time: 5 minutes**
- **Cook Time: 15 minutes**

Serves 4

¼ cup extra-virgin olive oil

4 medium Vidalia onions, sliced

4 cloves garlic, minced

1 tablespoon dried thyme

1 cup dry red wine

4 cups vegetable or mushroom broth

Pinch salt

Pinch freshly ground black pepper

4 slices French bread

4 ounces vegan mozzarella cheese, shredded

EXTRA HERBS

To add even more flavor to this rich, brothy soup, use a bouquet garni instead of just using thyme. Bouquet garni is a small bundle of herbs such as parsley, thyme, and bay tied together, often enclosed in a piece of cheesecloth. Remove the entire bouquet from the soup before serving.

1 Press the Sauté button on the Instant Pot® and add the olive oil. Sauté the onions until golden brown. Add the garlic and sauté 1 minute.

2 Add the thyme, wine, and broth to the pot and lock the lid into place. Press the Manual button and adjust timer to 12 minutes. When the timer beeps, let pressure release naturally until float valve drops and then unlock lid. Add the salt and pepper.

3 Preheat the oven to the broiler setting. Lightly toast the bread in a toaster.

4 Ladle the soup into oven-safe serving bowls and place the bowls on a large baking sheet. Place a slice of toasted bread on top of the soup in each bowl and sprinkle the cheese on top of the bread. Place the baking sheet in the oven and broil until the cheese melts.

Corn Chowder

For an extra kick you won't often find in chowder of any kind, drain, dice and add 2 (4-ounce) cans green chilies to this chowder. From there you're on your way to a kind of all-American fusion of New England chowder, a baked potato, and corn-tortilla soup.

- **Hands-On Time: 5 minutes**
- **Cook Time: 15 minutes**

Serves 6

2 tablespoons vegan margarine

4 large leeks

4 cups vegetable broth

2 cups water

1½ cups fresh or frozen corn kernels

6 medium russet or Idaho baking potatoes, peeled and diced

1 bay leaf

Pinch salt

Pinch freshly ground black pepper

½ teaspoon dried thyme

Pinch granulated sugar

½ cup unsweetened soy milk

1   Press the Sauté button on the Instant Pot® and melt the margarine. Cut off the root end of the leeks and discard any bruised outer leaves. Slice the leeks. Add the leeks to the pot and sauté 2 minutes.

2   Add the broth, water, corn, potatoes, bay leaf, salt, and pepper to the pot. Lock the lid into place, press the Manual button, and adjust timer to 10 minutes. When the timer beeps, quick-release pressure until float valve drops and then unlock lid.

3   Discard the bay leaf. Stir in the thyme, sugar, and soy milk. Use an immersion blender to blend until desired thickness and consistency is achieved. Serve hot.

WHAT IS CHOWDER?

Chowder means a thick soup made with chunks of seafood, but the meaning has been expanded to include other main ingredients, like vegetables such as corn.

White Bean with Garlic and Kale Soup

This dish is most often enjoyed during the winter, when kale is in peak season, but the increasingly popularity of kale makes it a rejuvenating and surprisingly hearty meal year-round. Try White Bean with Garlic and Kale Soup with your favorite vegan bread.

- **Hands-On Time: 5 minutes**
- **Cook Time: 11 minutes**

Serves 8

2 tablespoons olive oil

½ cup thinly sliced yellow onion

6 cloves garlic, thinly sliced

2 cups dried cannellini beans, soaked in water 8 hours

2 teaspoons dried oregano

1 (6-ounce) can tomato paste

2 tablespoons red wine vinegar

8 cups vegetable broth

3 cups chopped kale

Pinch salt

Pinch freshly ground black pepper

WHITE BEANS
Cannellini, great northern, and navy are all types of white beans. Each has its own unique flavor. Cannellini are the largest and have an earthy flavor.

1 Press the Sauté button on the Instant Pot® and add the oil. Add the onion and sauté until golden brown. Add the garlic and sauté about 1 minute.

2 Stir the remaining ingredients into the pot. Lock the lid into place, press the Manual button, and adjust the timer to 10 minutes. When the timer beeps, let pressure release naturally until float valve drops and then unlock lid.

3 Taste for seasoning and add more salt and pepper if needed. Serve warm.

Old-Fashioned Potato Soup

In this recipe the Instant Pot®'s handy Sauté function makes what might otherwise be a headache-inducing slew of dirty dishes into a one-pot meal. This Old-Fashioned Potato Soup can be stretched and made heartier by topping with soy bacon bits and shredded vegan cheese—voilà, it's now a baked potato soup!

- **Hands-On Time: 10 minutes**
- **Cook Time: 22 minutes**

Serves 4

¼ cup extra-virgin olive oil
½ cup diced yellow onion
½ cup sliced celery
4 cups peeled and diced
    Idaho or russet potatoes
3 cups vegetable broth
2 cups Béchamel Sauce (see
    recipe in Chapter 4)
Pinch salt
Pinch freshly ground black
    pepper
¼ cup chopped fresh chives
    or parsley (optional)

1 Press the Sauté button on the Instant Pot® and add the oil. Sauté the onion and celery about 5 minutes.

2 Add the potatoes and broth to the pot and lock the lid into place. Press the Manual button and adjust timer to 12 minutes. When the timer beeps, let pressure release naturally until float valve drops and then unlock lid.

3 Press the Sauté button on the pot and adjust setting to Low. Bring the soup to a simmer and slowly stir in the Béchamel Sauce until thickened, about 5 minutes. Add salt and pepper.

4 If desired, garnish with chives or parsley and serve warm.

Creamy Asparagus Soup

Asparagus soup is rich and satisfying in almost any preparation. This Creamy Asparagus Soup adds in a hint of cayenne to take things to a whole new level—add a bit more to kick it up even higher. To sneak some extra protein into this soup, try adding 1 cup cooked navy beans—or any other white bean—to the soup before blending.

- **Hands-On Time: 5 minutes**
- **Cook Time: 12 minutes**

Serves 4

2 pounds asparagus

2 tablespoons vegan margarine

1 large Vidalia onion, peeled and diced

1½ teaspoons salt

⅛ teaspoon cayenne pepper

5 cups vegetable broth

¼ cup unsweetened soy milk

1 teaspoon fresh lemon juice

PEAK SEASON

Asparagus is in peak season during the spring, and during this time there are plenty of the flavorful stalks for sale at grocery stores or farmers' markets. Use asparagus in a soup, grilled or baked, or even battered and fried.

1 Snap off and discard the hard ends of the asparagus spears. Cut the spears into 1" pieces.

2 Press the Sauté button on the Instant Pot® and add the margarine. Add the onion and sauté until golden brown. Add the asparagus, salt, and cayenne pepper; sauté about 5 minutes until the asparagus begins to soften.

3 Add the broth to the pot and lock the lid into place. Press the Manual button and adjust timer to 7 minutes. When the timer beeps, let pressure release naturally until float valve drops and then unlock lid.

4 Add the soy milk and lemon juice to the soup and purée using an immersion blender until desired consistency is achieved. Serve warm.

Cream of Mushroom Soup

Puréed potatoes bring substantial thickness to any creamy vegan soup. Your Instant Pot® can do the same with cauliflower, broccoli, or other similar vegetables. This dish features a small amount of white wine—if you need to sub it out, try a mushroom or vegetable broth.

- **Hands-On Time: 5 minutes**
- **Cook Time: 15 minutes**

Serves 4

¼ cup vegan margarine

1 medium yellow onion, peeled and diced

2 cups sliced button mushrooms

2 medium Idaho or russet potatoes, peeled and diced

2 cloves garlic, minced

¼ cup dry white wine

3 cups unsweetened soy milk

1 teaspoon dried thyme

3 cups Béchamel Sauce (see recipe in Chapter 4)

Pinch salt

Pinch freshly ground black pepper

1 Press the Sauté button on the Instant Pot® and add the margarine. Add the onions and sauté until golden brown. Add the mushrooms, potatoes, and garlic and continue sautéing about 5 minutes.

2 Add the white wine, soy milk, thyme, and Béchamel Sauce to the pot. Lock the lid into place, press the Manual button, and adjust timer to 10 minutes. When the timer beeps, let pressure release naturally until float valve drops and then unlock lid.

3 Purée the soup in the pot using an immersion blender until desired consistency is achieved. Season with salt and pepper. Serve warm.

VARIATIONS

This soup has mild flavors that are perfect as a base for additional flavors. Try adding vegetables, such as steamed green beans or spinach, or chunks of vegan chicken, for a cream of "chicken" soup.

Tortilla Soup

Tortilla Soup is well known but not as widely enjoyed as it probably should be outside of the immediate southern border states. This soup is a complete meal once you add avocado slices, and you can make it even heartier with cooked vegan chicken substitutes, such as MorningStar Farms Meal Starters Chik'n Strips.

- **Hands-On Time: 10 minutes**
- **Cook Time: 30 minutes**

Serves 6

2 tablespoons olive oil

1 large yellow onion, peeled and chopped

12 ounces firm silken tofu, crumbled

2 cloves garlic, minced

2 tablespoons soy sauce

7 cups vegetable broth

2 cups diced tomato

1 cup corn kernels

1 teaspoon chipotle powder

1 teaspoon cayenne pepper

2 teaspoons ground cumin

2 teaspoons salt

1 teaspoon dried oregano

10 (6") corn tortillas

8 ounces shredded vegan Cheddar cheese

CHIPOTLE POWDER

Chipotle powder is made from ground chipotle peppers, a type of dried jalapeño. It brings a smoky spiciness to dishes but can be replaced with cayenne pepper or chili powder.

1 Preheat oven to 450°F.

2 Press the Sauté button on the Instant Pot® and add the olive oil. Add the onions and sauté until just beginning to soften, and add tofu to combine and cook through, about 3 minutes. Add the garlic and sauté an additional 30 seconds.

3 Add the soy sauce, broth, tomato, corn, chipotle powder, cayenne, cumin, salt, and oregano to the pot; stir to combine. Lock the lid into place, press the Manual button on the pot, and adjust timer to 15 minutes. When the timer beeps, quick-release pressure until float valve drops and then unlock lid.

4 While the soup is cooking, slice the corn tortillas into thin strips and place on an ungreased baking sheet. Bake 10 minutes or until golden brown. Remove from heat and set aside.

5 Use an immersion blender or a regular blender to purée the soup in the pot.

6 Serve with cooked tortilla strips and 1 ounce shredded cheese on each bowl of soup.

Carrot Soup

Carrots are loaded with vitamin A and help maintain good vision, and those cooking for kids know that few foods this healthy and simple are this popular at the dinner table. In recent years, white, purple, and other colorful carrot varieties have been gaining shelf space in our grocery stores. Experiment with these colors and their subtle but discernable flavor profiles.

- **Hands-On Time: 5 minutes**
- **Cook Time: 20 minutes**

Serves 4

1 tablespoon olive oil

1 medium Vidalia onion, peeled and diced

2 cloves garlic, minced

3 teaspoons curry powder

1 bay leaf

1 pound carrots, peeled and chopped

2 cups vegetable broth

1 cup canned coconut milk

Pinch salt

Pinch freshly ground black pepper

¼ cup chiffonade basil

1   Press the Sauté button on the Instant Pot® and add the olive oil. Add the onions and sauté about 5 minutes until golden brown. Add the garlic and curry powder and sauté an additional 30 seconds.

2   Add the bay leaf, carrots, and broth to the pot. Lock the lid into place, press the Manual button, and adjust the timer to 15 minutes. When the timer beeps, let pressure release naturally until float valve drops and then unlock lid.

3   Remove the bay leaf. Use an immersion blender to purée the soup while slowly adding the coconut milk. Add salt and pepper. Garnish with basil before serving.

CHIFFONADE

Chiffonade is a technique for cutting herbs and greens. To chiffonade basil, stack the cleaned and dried leaves, roll them up loosely, and slice horizontally. You'll be left with thin ribbons of basil.

Black Bean and Lentil Chili

If you prefer a hotter chili, substitute a Scotch bonnet—also known as a Caribbean red pepper—or serrano pepper for the jalapeño. For a smokier dish, red wine can be mixed with the vegetable broth, or even substituted for it altogether.

- **Hands-On Time: 5 minutes**
- **Cook Time: 23 minutes**

Serves 6

2 tablespoons vegetable oil

1 large Spanish onion, peeled and diced

1 medium jalapeño, seeded and minced

1 clove garlic, minced

1 cup brown or green lentils

1 (15-ounce) can black beans, drained and rinsed

1 cup pearl barley

3 tablespoons chili powder

1 tablespoon sweet paprika

1 teaspoon dried oregano

1 teaspoon ground cumin

1 (28-ounce) can diced tomatoes

6 cups vegetable broth

1 jarred chipotle pepper in adobo sauce, minced (optional)

Pinch salt

Pinch freshly ground black pepper

1. Press the Sauté button on the Instant Pot® and add the oil. Add the onion and sauté 3 minutes. Stir in the jalapeño; sauté 1 minute. Stir in the garlic and sauté 30 seconds.

2. Stir the lentils, black beans, barley, chili powder, paprika, oregano, cumin, undrained tomatoes, and broth into the pot. If using, add the chipotle pepper along with some of the adobo sauce to taste. Lock the lid into place, press the Manual button, and adjust timer to 15 minutes. When the timer beeps, let pressure release naturally until float valve drops and then unlock lid.

3. Press the Sauté button on the pot and adjust setting to High. Bring to a simmer. Add salt and pepper and simmer until slightly thickened, about 3–5 minutes.

HANDLING PEPPERS

Hot peppers like jalapeño peppers must be handled carefully. Wear gloves while handling and wash your hands thoroughly once gloves are removed.

Vegetable Chili

Beans or no beans? The beans-in-chili debate rages on with no end in sight, but this recipe is so delicious that we're picking a side just this once. We call for canned beans here but dried can be used in your Instant Pot® for a meal loaded with even more protein, and it doesn't take that much more time to make than it does using canned beans.

- **Hands-On Time: 5 minutes**
- **Cook Time: 13 minutes**

Serves 8

2 tablespoons olive or vegetable oil

1 large sweet onion, peeled and diced

3 cloves garlic, minced

1 (15-ounce) can pinto beans, rinsed and drained

1 (15-ounce) can kidney beans, rinsed and drained

1 (15-ounce) can cannellini or other white beans, rinsed and drained

1 large green bell pepper, seeded and diced

2 cups diced zucchini

1½ cups corn kernels

1 (28-ounce) can diced tomatoes

2 cups vegetable broth

2 tablespoons chili powder

1 teaspoon ground cumin

1 teaspoon dried oregano

¼ teaspoon freshly ground black pepper

⅛ teaspoon cayenne pepper

Pinch salt (optional)

8 ounces vegan Monterey jack cheese, shredded

1   Press the Sauté button on the Instant Pot® and add the oil. Add the onion and sauté 3 minutes or until it begins to soften. Stir in the garlic and sauté 30 seconds.

2   Add the beans, bell pepper, zucchini, corn, tomatoes, broth, chili powder, cumin, oregano, black pepper, and cayenne pepper to the pot and stir to mix. Lock the lid into place, press the Manual button, and adjust timer to 9 minutes.

3   When the timer beeps, let pressure release naturally until float valve drops and then unlock lid. Stir the chili and add salt if desired. Serve topped with the shredded cheese.

Red Bean Chili

Use this basic chili recipe as the foundation for your own creation and add a variety of vegetables or faux meats while cooking. The Instant Pot® is a chili cook's godsend; in this recipe and many other it reduces the overall time investment by as much as two-thirds. For a change of pace, try this chili over white or brown rice.

- **Hands-On Time: 5 minutes**
- **Cook Time: 40 minutes**

Serves 4

1 tablespoon olive oil
½ cup yellow diced onion
2 cloves garlic, minced
2 cups dried kidney beans
8 cups water
8 cups vegetable broth
1 tablespoon chili powder
½ tablespoon chipotle powder
½ tablespoon ground cumin
½ tablespoon paprika
2 cups diced fresh tomatoes
2 teaspoons salt

1 Press the Sauté button on the Instant Pot® and heat the oil. Add the onions and sauté about 3 minutes. Add the garlic and cook an additional 30 seconds. Transfer the onion mixture to a small glass bowl and set aside.

2 Add the beans and water to the pot. Lock the lid into place, press the Bean button, and cook for the default time of 30 minutes. When the timer beeps, quick-release pressure until float valve drops and then unlock lid.

3 Add the onion mixture and all remaining ingredients to the pot. Lock the lid into place, press the Manual button, and adjust timer to 5 minutes. When the timer beeps, let pressure release naturally until float valve drops and then unlock lid.

4 If the desired consistency has not been reached, press the Sauté button on the pot and adjust setting to Low to simmer the chili until desired consistency is achieved.

Speedy Chili con "Carne"

Try Boca Veggie Ground Crumbles in this fast recipe as a vegan alternative to ground beef. Other brands and compositions abound, but whichever you choose, try to stick with that brand until you've made this dish a couple of times. You'll find that the crumble varies by brand and burger style, and with practice you'll find the right texture for your table.

- **Hands-On Time: 5 minutes**
- **Cook Time: 17 minutes**

Serves 4

1 tablespoon olive oil
½ cup diced yellow onion
½ cup diced green bell pepper
1 (12-ounce) package frozen veggie burger crumbles
2 cloves garlic, minced
1 (15-ounce) can kidney beans, rinsed and drained
2 cups vegetable broth
1 tablespoon chili powder
½ tablespoon chipotle powder
½ tablespoon ground cumin
1 teaspoon dried thyme
1 tablespoon dried oregano
2 cups diced fresh tomatoes
1 tablespoon tomato paste
1 tablespoon apple cider vinegar
2 teaspoons salt

1 Press the Sauté button on the Instant Pot® and add the oil. Add the onions and bell pepper and sauté about 3 minutes. Add the burger crumbles and garlic and cook until the crumbles are heated through, about 3–4 minutes.

2 Add all remaining ingredients to the pot. Lock the lid into place, press the Manual button, and adjust timer to 10 minutes. When the timer beeps, let pressure release naturally until float valve drops and then unlock lid.

3 If the desired consistency has not been reached, press the Sauté button on the pot and adjust setting to Low. Simmer the chili until the desired consistency is achieved.

VEGAN BEEF

You can also try Gimme Lean Ground Beef Style for a prepackaged option, or rehydrated texturized vegetable protein (TVP).

Irish "Beef" Stew

Surprisingly, not all beers are safe for vegan consumption. Guinness is a popular Irish stout, but it is treated with isinglass finings made from fish and so must not be used in this stew. There are plenty of beer substitutes out there for those who are avoiding it, but trust us: for this dish, you'll want to use a mushroom broth.

- **Hands-On Time: 5 minutes**
- **Cook Time: 35 minutes**

Serves 5

2 tablespoons olive oil

1 pound cooked seitan, cut into 1" cubes

2 medium carrots, peeled and sliced

1 medium yellow onion, peeled and diced

2 cloves garlic, minced

3 tablespoons all-purpose flour

1 pound russet potatoes, cubed

6 cups faux beef broth

1 cup vegan Irish stout beer

1 cup dry red wine

2 tablespoons tomato paste

1 tablespoon granulated sugar

1 tablespoon dried thyme

1 tablespoon vegan Worcestershire sauce

1 bay leaf

1 teaspoon salt

½ teaspoon freshly ground black pepper

1 Press the Sauté button on the Instant Pot® and add the olive oil. Add the seitan, carrots, and onion and sauté until just soft, about 5 minutes. Stir in the garlic and flour and sauté an additional 30 seconds.

2 Add all remaining ingredients to the pot. Lock the lid into place, press the Manual button, and adjust timer to 30 minutes. When the timer beeps, let pressure release naturally until float valve drops and then unlock lid.

3 Remove the bay leaf before serving.

Brunswick Stew

This stew is served from huge cast-iron pots at fairs and festivals in the American South; your Instant Pot® will make for much easier cleanup. Original or hickory smoked barbecue sauce works best in this recipe. As always, remember to check the label to ensure your sauce is free of animal products.

- **Hands-On Time: 5 minutes**
- **Cook Time: 35 minutes**

Serves 4

2 tablespoons olive oil

1 medium onion, peeled and chopped

2 medium stalks celery, sliced

1 medium bell pepper, seeded and diced

1 (16-ounce) package vegan chicken chunks

1 (28-ounce) can crushed tomatoes

2 cups corn kernels

1 cup ketchup

½ cup barbecue sauce

1 tablespoon liquid smoke

1 tablespoon vegan Worcestershire sauce

1 teaspoon salt

½ teaspoon freshly ground black pepper

1 Press the Sauté button on the Instant Pot® and add the olive oil. Sauté the onions, celery, and bell pepper until soft, about 5 minutes. Add the vegan chicken and cook until done according to package directions, about 3–5 minutes.

2 Add all remaining ingredients to the pot. Lock the lid into place, press the Manual button, and adjust timer to 30 minutes. When the timer beeps, let pressure release naturally until float valve drops and then unlock lid.

RECIPE ORIGINS

Competing cities both claim to be the originator of this popular southern stew. Both Brunswick, Georgia, and Brunswick County, Virginia, take credit for creating this recipe.

Oyster Mushroom Stew

Oyster mushrooms are highly recommended because of their delicate texture—many say it mimics that of fish—but this slow-cooking stew can be made with just about any kind of white mushroom. Brown varietals shouldn't necessarily be avoided, but they'll alter the flavor profile enough to make this a different dish in spirit.

- **Hands-On Time: 5 minutes**
- **Cook Time: 35 minutes**

Serves 4

2 tablespoons vegan margarine
½ cup diced yellow onions
½ cup diced celery
1 clove garlic, minced
½ cup Béchamel Sauce (see recipe in Chapter 4)
1 pound oyster mushrooms, chopped
½ cup dry white wine
2 cups unsweetened soy milk
½ teaspoon dried thyme
1 teaspoon salt
1 teaspoon fresh lemon juice
½ cup chopped parsley (optional)

1 Press the Sauté button on the Instant Pot® and heat the margarine. Add the onions and celery and sauté 5 minutes. Add the garlic and sauté an additional 30 seconds.

2 Add the Béchamel Sauce, mushrooms, wine, soy milk, thyme, and salt to the pot. Lock the lid into place, press the Manual button, and adjust timer to 30 minutes. When the timer beeps, let pressure release naturally until float valve drops and then unlock lid.

3 If a thicker consistency is desired, press the Sauté button on the pot and adjust setting to Low. Simmer until desired consistency is achieved. Stir in the lemon juice.

4 Stir in chopped parsley before serving if desired.

6

Rice, Grains, and Potatoes

Tired of soaking your grains overnight? Tired of eating highly processed rice and grains so that they will cook quicker? Fortunately, your Instant Pot® can solve these problems and you'll be eating rice and grains in no time. Be sure to carefully follow the recipe instructions in this chapter as the rice, grains, and potatoes continue to cook in the steam during the pressure-release phase of Instant Pot® cooking. If you release the pressure too early, it could result in inedible little pebbles. Plus, starchy items can clog up the antiblock shield if the pressure is released too quickly. So plug in your Instant Pot® and get ready to enjoy recipes such as Wild Mushroom Risotto, Vegan Chorizo Paella, Scalloped Potatoes, Three-Grain Pilaf, and more.

Garlic Parsley Mashed Potatoes

Did you know that russet potatoes are also commonly called Idaho potatoes? If ever the Instant Pot® made a dish not just quicker but much easier to prepare, this has to be it. It's tempting for many cooks to skip the parsley, but try this dish with it. This much-maligned herb is not tasteless as many assume, but is in fact mildly bitter and adds flavor to savory dishes in a way similar to that of a dash of pepper or a squeeze of lemon.

- **Hands-On Time: 5 minutes**
- **Cook Time: 8 minutes**

Serves 6

1 cup water

8 cups quartered russet potatoes, peeled if preferred

½ medium yellow onion, peeled and diced

4 cloves garlic, minced

¼ cup vegan margarine

½ cup unsweetened almond milk or unsweetened soy milk

½ cup chopped fresh Italian flat-leaf parsley

2 teaspoons salt

½ teaspoon freshly ground black pepper

1 Pour the water into the Instant Pot® and add the potatoes, onion, and garlic; stir to combine. Lock the lid into place. Press the Manual button and adjust timer to 8 minutes. When the timer beeps, let pressure release naturally for 10 minutes. Quick-release any remaining pressure until float valve drops and then unlock lid.

2 Add the margarine and almond milk to the pot and mash the potatoes using a potato masher or electric mixer.

3 Mix in the parsley, salt, and pepper, and serve.

Rosemary Mashed Potatoes

These basic flavors can be used in other potato dishes if you're not in the mood for mashed potatoes. Try roasting quartered red potatoes or whole fingerlings with rosemary, salt, and pepper. That said, it's not unlikely that Rosemary Mashed Potatoes in the Instant Pot® will become your go-to preparation of this classic dish.

- **Hands-On Time: 5 minutes**
- **Cook Time: 8 minutes**

Serves 6

1 cup water

8 cups peeled and quartered russet potatoes

1 tablespoon chopped fresh rosemary

4 cloves garlic, minced

¼ cup vegan margarine

1 cup unsweetened almond milk or unsweetened soy milk

2 teaspoons salt

½ teaspoon freshly ground black pepper

1 Pour the water into the Instant Pot® and add the potatoes, rosemary, and garlic; stir to combine. Lock the lid into place. Press the Manual button and adjust timer to 8 minutes. When the timer beeps, let pressure release naturally for 10 minutes. Quick-release any remaining pressure until float valve drops and then unlock lid.

2 Add the margarine and almond milk to the pot and mash the potatoes using a potato masher or electric mixer.

3 Mix in the salt and pepper, and serve.

GROWING ROSEMARY

Rosemary is one of the easiest herbs to grow and is the perfect addition to any herb garden. It can grow year-round and does not need constant sunlight.

Mediterranean Sweet Potato Salad

Serve this salad at room temperature or refrigerate it for a few hours and served chilled. Note: "room temperature" is understood to be within the range of a living or dining room in a climate-controlled building. If the temperature in your room is above 73 degrees, by all means chill this salad!

- **Hands-On Time: 5 minutes**
- **Cook Time: 15 minutes**

Serves 4

¼ cup olive oil

1 medium yellow onion, peeled and diced

2 cloves garlic, minced

1 teaspoon ground cumin

1 teaspoon paprika

¼ cup fresh lemon juice

1 cup water

3 cups peeled and cubed sweet potatoes

¼ cup chopped green olives

3 tablespoons chopped fresh Italian flat-leaf parsley

Pinch salt

Pinch freshly ground black pepper

1 Add the olive oil to the Instant Pot® and press the Sauté button. Add the onion and sauté until it begins to turn golden brown. Add the garlic, cumin, paprika, and lemon juice; cook about 2 minutes. Transfer to a large bowl and set aside.

2 Add the water and the sweet potatoes to the pot. Lock the lid into place, press the Manual button, and adjust timer to 10 minutes. When the timer beeps, let pressure release naturally until float valve drops and then unlock lid.

3 Drain the sweet potatoes in a colander. Toss the potatoes with the onion mixture. Add the olives and parsley and season with salt and pepper, and serve warm.

Chipotle and Thyme Mashed Sweet Potatoes

This is a rare and enticing version of mashed potatoes, one so much more fragrant and, frankly, exciting than the traditional version that it hardly deserves to share the name. If you'd like to substitute fresh thyme for dried thyme in this Chipotle and Thyme Mashed Sweet Potatoes dish, use ½ tablespoon of the fresh herb.

- **Hands-On Time: 10 minutes**
- **Cook Time: 10 minutes**

Serves 4

2 cups water

6 cups peeled and cubed sweet potatoes

¼ cup vegan margarine

3 cloves garlic, minced

½ teaspoon dried chipotle pepper

½ teaspoon dried thyme

Pinch salt

Pinch freshly ground black pepper

1 Pour the water into the Instant Pot® and add the sweet potatoes, margarine, and garlic. Lock the lid into place, press the Manual button, and adjust timer to 10 minutes.

2 When the timer beeps, let pressure release naturally for 10 minutes. Quick-release any remaining pressure until float valve drops and then unlock lid.

3 Drain any remaining liquid from the pot and add the chipotle pepper and thyme. Mash the potatoes using a potato masher or electric mixer.

4 Season with salt and pepper and serve.

Mashed Sweet Potatoes

Turn these Mashed Sweet Potatoes into a sweet potato casserole by covering with vegan marshmallows, such as Sweet & Sara brand, and baking in an uncovered dish. Traditional marshmallows contain gelatin, which is made from animal skin and bones, so make sure you find the right ones.

- **Hands-On Time: 5 minutes**
- **Cook Time: 8 minutes**

Serves 3

1 cup water
¼ cup vegetable broth
5 cups peeled and cubed sweet potatoes
¼ cup vegan margarine
⅛ cup orange juice
2 tablespoons maple syrup
Pinch salt
Pinch freshly ground black pepper

RECIPE SUBSTITUTIONS

If you don't have pure maple syrup on hand, you can use inexpensive pancake syrup instead. It won't be as flavorful as pure maple syrup but it will do the job.

1 Pour the water and broth into the Instant Pot®. Add the sweet potatoes and stir to combine. Lock the lid into place. Press the Manual button and adjust timer to 8 minutes.

2 When the timer beeps, let pressure release naturally for 10 minutes. Quick-release any remaining pressure until float valve drops and then unlock lid.

3 Add the margarine, orange juice, and syrup to the pot and mash the potatoes using a potato masher or electric mixer.

4 Mix in the salt and pepper and serve.

Herbed Potatoes

Any combination of herbs will work in this simple potato side dish. A mix of rosemary, thyme, dill, and coriander is a great blend, and there are as many others as your pantry can suggest. Instant Pot® is up to the task of cooking 8 cups of potatoes in 15 minutes, but if you have the time there's no reason not to adjust the timing slightly and prepare this in two batches.

- **Hands-On Time: 5 minutes**
- **Cook Time: 15 minutes**

Serves 8

2 tablespoons olive oil

1 medium Vidalia onion, peeled and diced

8 cups quartered red potatoes

¼ cup water

1 teaspoon dried oregano

1 teaspoon dried basil

Pinch salt

Pinch freshly ground black pepper

1 Press the Sauté button on the Instant Pot® and add the olive oil. Add the onion and sauté 3 minutes or until softened.

2 Add the potatoes to the pan cut-side down. Fry uncovered 5 minutes or until they begin to brown. Pour in the water. Sprinkle the herbs over the potatoes.

3 Lock the lid into place, press the Manual button, and adjust timer to 7 minutes. When the timer beeps, let pressure release naturally until float valve drops and then unlock lid. Season with salt and pepper. Serve warm.

Potato Piccata

Piccata typically denotes a dish of Italian origin that contains butter, lemon, and herbs, but of course most vegans haven't had a good one since saying goodbye to chicken. You'll enjoy this vegan version, which is based on potatoes you won't have to spend all afternoon smashing!

- **Hands-On Time: 3 minutes**
- **Cook Time: 8 minutes**

Serves 4

2 tablespoons vegan margarine
1 medium yellow onion, peeled and julienned
1 medium red bell pepper, seeded and sliced
2 cups water
4 medium russet potatoes, peeled and sliced
¼ cup vegetable broth
2 tablespoons fresh lemon juice
¼ cup chopped fresh Italian flat-leaf parsley
Pinch salt
Pinch freshly ground black pepper

1 Press the Sauté button on the Instant Pot® and add the margarine. Add the onion and red pepper; sauté 3 minutes or until the onion is softened.

2 Add the water, potatoes, broth, and lemon juice. Lock the lid into place, press the Manual button, and adjust timer to 5 minutes. When the timer beeps, let pressure release naturally until float valve drops and then unlock lid.

3 Add the parsley and season with salt and pepper. Serve warm.

JULIENNE
Julienne is a type of cut that turns food into long, thin, matchstick-like pieces. Each julienned piece is typically ⅛"–¼" thick.

Potato Risotto

Risotto is typically made with Arborio rice; this recipe shows that the same technique can be applied to a finely diced potato for a unique twist on the russet, which is used primarily for french fries and mashed potatoes. As always, remember to substitute a vegetable broth–based liquid if any of your eaters is avoiding alcohol.

- **Hands-On Time: 9 minutes**
- **Cook Time: 14 minutes**

Serves 6

2 medium leeks (white part only)

¼ cup plus 1 tablespoon olive oil, divided

3 sprigs fresh thyme

3 pounds russet potatoes, peeled and diced into ⅛" cubes

½ cup dry white wine

2 cups mushroom broth

4 cups fresh spinach leaves

Pinch salt

Pinch freshly ground black pepper

1 Thinly slice leeks crosswise into semicircles and rinse. Press the Sauté button on the Instant Pot® and add ¼ cup olive oil. Add the leeks and sauté until translucent. Add the thyme and continue to sauté 4 minutes, then transfer to a medium bowl.

2 In the medium bowl, toss the potatoes with 1 tablespoon olive oil to thinly coat. Add the potatoes to the pot and sauté 5 minutes.

3 Add the wine and deglaze the pot, then cook until the wine has almost evaporated, about 2-4 minutes. Add the leek mixture and the broth to the potatoes in the pot. Lock the lid into place, press the Manual button, and adjust timer to 5 minutes. When the timer beeps, let pressure release naturally until float valve drops and then unlock lid.

4 Add the spinach to the pot and stir until it is wilted and all of the ingredients have been combined.

5 Season with salt and pepper and serve.

Scalloped Potatoes

Your Instant Pot® is great at taking traditionally baked dishes and steaming them instead—usually in much less time than you'd expect. The "hands-on" time listed here may vary depending on your deftness with the hyper-thin julienne-style cut, but once it's in the pot, the cooking time is cut at least in half from traditional preparation times.

- **Hands-On Time: 5 minutes**
- **Cook Time: 20 minutes**

Serves 4

2 tablespoons vegan margarine

½ cup julienned Vidalia onion

2 cloves garlic, minced

3 cups Béchamel Sauce (see recipe in Chapter 4)

1 teaspoon salt

¼ teaspoon freshly ground black pepper

1 cup water

4 large russet potatoes, peeled and thinly sliced

SCALLOPED

Scalloped traditionally means a dish that is covered in sauce and bread crumbs. You can skip the bread crumbs to make a crust out of a well-cooked sauce instead.

1. Press the Sauté button on the Instant Pot® and add the margarine. Add the onion and sauté until it begins to turn golden brown. Add the garlic and sauté 1 minute more. Add the Béchamel Sauce, salt, and pepper, and cook until the sauce has thickened. Transfer the mixture to a medium bowl and set aside. Rinse the Instant Pot® and spray with cooking spray.

2. Pour the water into the Instant Pot® and place half of the potatoes on the bottom of the pot. Cover the potatoes with half of the sauce. Add another layer of potatoes and sauce, and then cover.

3. Lock the lid into place, press the Manual button, and adjust timer to 15 minutes. When the timer beeps, let pressure release naturally until float valve drops and then unlock lid.

4. Season with additional salt and pepper if desired and serve.

Wild Mushroom Risotto

Exotic mushrooms such as shiitakes, hen of the woods, and oysters add earthy flavor and diverse textures that make Wild Mushroom Risotto a quick-and-delicious Instant Pot® showpiece. For a budget-friendly mushroom, choose any variety of white common mushroom. Cremini and other brown tops may push the flavor a bit too rich for some palates, but if rich and mushroomy is to your fancy, here's the dish for you!

- **Hands-On Time: 5 minutes**
- **Cook Time: 20 minutes**

Serves 6

1 tablespoon olive oil
½ medium yellow onion, peeled and diced
1 clove garlic, minced
2 cups Arborio rice
6 cups vegetable broth, divided
2 cups chopped assorted mushrooms
1 tablespoon vegan margarine
Pinch salt
Pinch freshly ground black pepper

RISOTTO TECHNIQUE
The technique used to make risotto results in a creamy consistency without the use of milk or soy milk. Instead, the creaminess is achieved by gradually adding broth to rice while stirring.

1 Press the Sauté button on the Instant Pot® and add the olive oil. Add the onion and sauté until just soft, about 3 minutes. Add the garlic and sauté an additional 30 seconds. Add the rice and sauté 4 minutes or until the rice becomes opaque.

2 Add 5 cups vegetable broth to the pot. Lock the lid into place, press the Manual button, and adjust timer to 6 minutes. When the timer beeps, quick-release pressure until float valve drops and then unlock lid.

3 Press the Sauté button on the pot and stir in the remaining broth and the mushrooms. Let the risotto simmer until the liquid is absorbed, about 5 minutes.

4 Add the margarine to the risotto and season with salt and pepper just before serving.

Brown Rice

There was a time not many decades ago when rice was available to most Americans only in a small box with a man's face on it, and maybe also in a cute 1-pound bag. No more, as many national grocers have adapted to our changing kitchens by offering white rice in containers up to 25 pounds. Instant Pot® has a designated setting for this, humanity's most universal dish.

- **Hands-On Time: 1 minute**
- **Cook Time: 40 minutes**

Serves 4

1 cup long-grain brown rice
1 teaspoon salt
2 cups water

1 Add the rice, salt, and water to the Instant Pot®. Lock the lid into place. Press the Rice button and let cook for the default time. When the timer beeps, let pressure release naturally until float valve drops and then unlock lid.

2 Fluff with a fork before serving or using in a recipe.

White Rice

White Rice has overtaken brown rice as the most widely consumed preparation worldwide, and in the United States it's not even close. White Rice requires a bit less water, but otherwise the Instant Pot® steps are the same. Rice accounts for more than 20 percent of the calories consumed worldwide.

- **Hands-On Time: 1 minute**
- **Cook Time: 40 minutes**

Serves 4

1 cup long-grain white rice
1½ cups water

1 Add the rice and water to the Instant Pot®. Lock the lid into place. Press the Rice button and let cook for the default time. When the timer beeps, let pressure release naturally until float valve drops and then unlock lid.

2 Fluff with a fork before serving or using in a recipe.

Quinoa

Quinoa, the once-mysterious, now-ubiquitous ancient grain many vegetarians and vegans would be hard-pressed to live without, contains all nine essential amino acids including lysine, which is rare in grains and is part of what makes this one so popular and so similar to animal proteins in its nutritional value.

- **Hands-On Time: 1 minute**
- **Cook Time: 20 minutes**

Serves 4

1 cup quinoa
2 cups water

1 Add the quinoa and water to the Instant Pot®. Lock the lid into place. Press the Multigrain button and let cook for the default time. When the timer beeps, let pressure release naturally until float valve drops and then unlock lid.

2 Fluff with a fork before serving or using in a recipe.

Couscous

Couscous is actually a kind of pasta. Made of tiny balls of semolina—the coarse wheat "middlings" or groats that are the precursor to many pastas—couscous is often served as a grain, with vegetables as a topping or on the side.

- **Hands-On Time: 1 minute**
- **Cook Time: 22 minutes**

Serves 4

1 cup couscous
2 cups water

1 Add the couscous and water to the Instant Pot®. Lock the lid into place, press the Manual button, and adjust the timer to 6 minutes. When the timer beeps, let pressure release naturally until float valve drops and then unlock lid.

2 Fluff with a fork before serving or using in a recipe.

Barley Risotto

Vegan cheeses are becoming more readily available at even the larger national grocery chains. Finding one to suit your own taste is essential for this risotto. Barley has a thin-yet-savory quality all its own, but you'll want a flavorful vegan cheese for balance.

- **Hands-On Time: 5 minutes**
- **Cook Time: 23 minutes**

Serves 4

1 tablespoon vegan margarine

1 tablespoon olive oil

1 large yellow onion, peeled and diced

1 clove garlic, minced

1 medium stalk celery, finely minced

1½ cups pearl barley, well rinsed

⅓ cup dried cremini mushrooms

4 cups vegetable broth

2¼ cups water

1 cup grated vegan Parmesan cheese

2 tablespoons minced fresh Italian flat-leaf parsley

Pinch salt

1 Press the Sauté button on the Instant Pot®. Add the margarine, oil, and onion; sauté 3 minutes or until the onion is soft. Add the garlic and sauté 30 seconds. Stir in the celery and barley until the barley is coated with oil.

2 Add the mushrooms, broth, and water. Lock the lid into place, press the Manual button, and set timer to 18 minutes. When the timer beeps, quick-release pressure until float valve drops and then unlock lid.

3 Drain off any excess liquid not absorbed by the barley, leaving just enough to leave the risotto slightly soupy. Press the Sauté button and adjust setting to Low.

4 When risotto is cooked thoroughly, stir in the cheese and parsley. Add salt and serve.

FLAVOR VARIATIONS

To further enhance the earthy flavor of the mushrooms and barley, add ½ teaspoon dried thyme and ½ teaspoon dried sage instead of fresh parsley.

Peppery Brown Rice Risotto

If anyone at your table is avoiding alcohol, you can simply replace the white wine in this recipe with ¼ cup vegetable broth. A half-broth, half-vinegar mixture also works well in this Peppery Brown Rice Risotto, which looks, smells, and tastes of springtime.

- **Hands-On Time: 5 minutes**
- **Cook Time: 23 minutes**

Serves 8

2 medium leeks

1 small fennel bulb

3 tablespoons vegan margarine

2 cups short-grain brown rice, rinsed and drained

½ teaspoon salt

2½ cups water

¼ cup dry white wine

¾ cup vegan Parmesan cheese

1½ teaspoons freshly ground black pepper

1 Cut the leeks into quarters lengthwise, and then slice into ½" slices.

2 Trim the fronds from the fennel, chop, and set aside. Dice the bulb.

3 Press Sauté on the Instant Pot® and melt the margarine. Add the leeks and fennel bulb; sauté 1 minute or until the leeks begin to wilt.

4 Add the rice and stir-fry until the rice begins to turn golden brown.

5 Stir the salt, water, and wine into the pot. Lock the lid into place, press the Manual button, and adjust timer to 20 minutes.

6 When the timer beeps, let pressure release naturally for 10 minutes. Quick-release any remaining pressure until float valve drops and then unlock lid.

7 Fluff the rice with a fork. Stir in the cheese, fennel fronds, and pepper. Serve warm.

Pumpkin Risotto

This seasonal Pumpkin Risotto will make for a welcome entrée on any Thanksgiving table, vegan or otherwise. It's a bit of extra work, but you may want to purée your own pumpkin in a food processor or blender for an even fresher autumn flavor. Whatever you do, don't skimp on the ginger and nutmeg.

- **Hands-On Time: 5 minutes**
- **Cook Time: 25 minutes**

Serves 6

1 tablespoon olive oil

1 cup diced sweet yellow onion

2 cups Arborio rice

1 cup dry white wine

2 cups vegetable broth

2 cups water, divided

1 cup canned pumpkin purée

1 teaspoon grated fresh ginger

1 teaspoon grated fresh nutmeg

Pinch salt

Pinch freshly ground black pepper

1 Press the Sauté button on the Instant Pot® and heat the olive oil. Add the onion and sauté about 4 minutes or until translucent. Add the rice and sauté until opaque, about 4 minutes.

2 Add the wine and stir until the liquid is reduced, about 7 minutes. Add the vegetable broth and 1 cup water. Lock the lid into place, press the Manual button, and adjust timer to 6 minutes. When the timer beeps, quick-release pressure until float valve drops and then unlock lid.

3 Add the remaining water, pumpkin purée, ginger, and nutmeg. Press the Sauté button on the pot and simmer ingredients until the liquid is absorbed.

4 Season with salt and pepper before serving.

Bulgur Stuffing

Bulgur, a cereal of mixed grains originally found in Armenian and Middle Eastern cooking, is a healthier alternative to white bread in stuffing. Note that depending on your local conditions—particularly altitude—you may find slightly less liquid makes for a better bite.

- **Hands-On Time: 10 minutes**
- **Cook Time: 20 minutes**

Serves 4

2 tablespoons vegan margarine
½ medium yellow onion, peeled and diced
½ cup diced celery
½ cup chopped button mushrooms
½ teaspoon dried thyme
½ teaspoon dried sage
½ teaspoon salt
¾ teaspoon freshly ground black pepper
1 cup bulgur
3 cups vegetable broth

1 Press the Sauté button on the Instant Pot® and melt the margarine. Add the onion and celery and sauté until soft, about 7 minutes. Add the mushrooms, thyme, sage, salt, and pepper, and sauté an additional 2 minutes. Transfer mixture to a small bowl and set aside.

2 Add the bulgur and broth to the pot. Lock the lid into place, press the manual button, and adjust timer to 9 minutes. When the timer beeps, let pressure release naturally until float valve drops and then unlock lid.

3 Pour the vegetable mixture into the cooked bulgur and stir until well combined.

TASTY SUBSTITUTIONS
Turn this dish into a cranberry stuffing by adding dried cranberries and chopped pecan pieces instead of the mushrooms and celery.

Vegetable Rice Pilaf

A pilaf can be any rice dish cooked in a seasoned broth, and as such the name has attached itself to a vast range of meals, including a great many available in the pre-prepared grocery aisle. Don't be fooled: instant pilaf and Instant Pot® pilaf have nothing in common but the name—with a marginal difference in prep time, you'll never go back to that cardboard supermarket stuff.

- **Hands-On Time: 5 minutes**
- **Cook Time: 12 minutes**

Serves 4

1 tablespoon vegan margarine

1 tablespoon vegetable oil

½ small yellow onion, peeled and thinly sliced

2 cloves garlic, minced

1½" piece fresh ginger, peeled and grated

1 medium serrano pepper, seeded and minced

1½ cups quartered cauliflower florets

1 cup green bean pieces (about 1" pieces)

½ cup peeled and diagonally sliced carrots

1 teaspoon ground cumin

½ teaspoon turmeric powder

¼ teaspoon cardamom seeds

1 teaspoon chili powder

⅛ teaspoon ground cloves

⅛ teaspoon hot paprika

½ teaspoon salt

1 cup long-grain white rice

1½ cups water

¼ cup slivered almonds, toasted

1. Press the Sauté button on the Instant Pot® and melt the margarine. Add the oil, onion, garlic, ginger, and serrano pepper; sauté 2 minutes.

2. Add the cauliflower, green beans, carrot, cumin, turmeric, cardamom, chili powder, cloves, paprika, salt, rice, and water to the pot and stir to mix. Lock the lid into place, press the Manual button, and adjust timer to 9 minutes.

3. When the timer beeps, let pressure release naturally for 15 minutes. Quick-release any remaining pressure until float valve drops and then unlock lid.

4. Fluff rice with a fork. Transfer to a serving bowl, top with toasted almonds, and serve.

Three-Grain Pilaf

Millet, which is essentially a grass and is indigenous to semiarid tropical regions around the world, is a good source of both protein and B vitamins.

- **Hands-On Time: 5 minutes**
- **Cook Time: 12 minutes**

Serves 4

2 tablespoons extra-virgin olive oil

½ cup sliced green onions

1 cup jasmine rice

½ cup millet

½ cup quinoa

2½ cups vegetable broth or water

Pinch salt

Pinch freshly ground black pepper

1 Press the Sauté button on the Instant Pot® and add the olive oil. Add the green onions and sauté 2–3 minutes. Add the grains and sauté 2–3 minutes more.

2 Add the broth or water to the pot and bring to a boil. Lock the lid into place, press the Manual button, and adjust timer to 6 minutes.

3 When the timer beeps, let pressure release naturally for 5 minutes. Quick-release any remaining pressure until float valve drops and then unlock lid.

4 Fluff the pilaf with a fork. Add salt and pepper. Serve warm.

Chinese Black Rice

Chinese black rice—once called "Forbidden Rice" as only royalty were permitted to consume it—can be used in savory or sweet dishes. Contrary to wide assumption, it does indeed grow black, and is a great source of iron and vitamin E.

- **Hands-On Time: 2 minutes**
- **Cook Time: 25 minutes**

Serves 4

1 cup Chinese black rice

2 cups vegetable broth

1 teaspoon rice wine vinegar

1 teaspoon Chinese five-spice powder

½ teaspoon salt

1 Press the Rice button on the Instant Pot® and add the rice and broth. Lock the lid into place and let cook for the default time. When the timer beeps, let pressure release naturally until float valve drops and then unlock lid.

2 Stir in the vinegar, five-spice powder, and salt. Fluff the rice with a fork.

Vegan Chorizo Paella

Chorizo here refers to the Spanish sausage, not the Mexican version. They are vastly different in flavor and texture, so be sure to seek out the right substitute. The Trader Joe's grocery store chain carries a delicious kind of vegan chorizo sausage, and other great brands can be found at your nearest health-conscious grocery store.

- **Hands-On Time: 10 minutes**
- **Cook Time: 20 minutes**

Serves 4

¼ cup olive oil

14 ounces vegetarian chorizo sausage, cut into 1" slices

1 cup diced yellow onion

4 cloves garlic, minced

½ cup chopped fresh Italian flat-leaf parsley, divided

1 (14.5-ounce) can diced tomatoes, drained

1 cup peeled and grated carrots

1 medium red bell pepper, seeded and chopped

1 cup fresh or frozen green peas

1½ teaspoons turmeric powder

1 cup basmati rice

2 cups vegetable broth

Pinch salt

Pinch freshly ground black pepper

1 Press the Sauté button on the Instant Pot® and add the oil. Sauté the "sausage" until it is browned, about 6 minutes. Transfer the sausage to a small bowl and set aside.

2 Add the onion, garlic, half the parsley, tomatoes, carrot, bell pepper, peas, and turmeric to the pot; sauté 3–5 minutes.

3 Add the rice, broth, and sausage to the pot. Lock the lid into place, press the Manual button, and adjust the timer to 9 minutes. When the timer beeps, let pressure release naturally until float valve drops and then unlock lid.

4 Garnish with the rest of the parsley. Season with salt and pepper before serving.

Creole Jambalaya

Jambalaya is a quintessentially New World dish, with roots in Provence and eastern Spain that have marinated for centuries in the flavors of Louisiana. Try MorningStar Farms Meal Starter Chik'n Strips and Tofurky sausage to add depth of savory flavor to this classic bayou-country dish.

- **Hands-On Time: 10 minutes**
- **Cook Time: 16 minutes**

Serves 8

½ cup vegan margarine
1 cup chopped white onion
1 medium green bell pepper, seeded and chopped
2 medium stalks celery, chopped
3 cloves garlic, minced
3 cups vegetable broth
1 cup water
1 cup tomato sauce
2 cups long-grain white rice
2 bay leaves
2 teaspoons dried thyme
2 teaspoons cayenne pepper
2 teaspoons Cajun seasoning
2 cups cooked vegan chicken and sausage (optional)
Pinch salt

1 Press the Sauté button on the Instant Pot® and melt the margarine. Add the onion, bell pepper, celery, and garlic and sauté about 10 minutes until soft.

2 Add the broth, water, tomato sauce, rice, bay leaves, thyme, cayenne, and Cajun seasoning to the pot and stir to combine. Lock the lid into place, press the Manual button, and adjust timer to 6 minutes. When the timer beeps, let pressure release naturally until float valve drops and then unlock lid.

3 Remove bay leaves. Stir in the prepared chopped vegan chicken and sausage, if using, and let stand 5 minutes. Season with salt.

CREOLE CUISINE
Creole cuisine is similar to, but more refined than, Cajun cooking, and both use the Holy Trinity of onion, bell pepper, and celery as the base of many dishes. It hails from southern Louisiana, but is influenced by Spanish, French, and African cuisines.

Beans

There is nothing better suited for the Instant Pot® than beans. No longer will you have to endure hours of waiting for your dried beans to soak. Now instead you can have beans in minutes, without having to open a can. Refried beans in under an hour, lentils in only 30 minutes—the Instant Pot® is sure to be your new go-to bean cooker. It is important to note however, that while beans and legumes are less prone to being overcooked in an Instant Pot® they can be undercooked, resulting in a hard and unpleasant dish. Letting the pressure release naturally will help ensure that your beans turn out tender and delicious. With recipes ranging from New Orleans Red Beans and Rice to Lentil-Spinach Curry, and simple recipes for cooking every type of bean you can imagine, this chapter will help get you started on some invaluable Instant Pot® bean recipes.

Pinto Beans

Most beans must be soaked for at least 4 hours before cooking, and pinto beans—for many the elemental cornerstone of Mexican and Central American cooking—are no different. With your Instant Pot®, you can try the "quick soak" described in this recipe.

- **Hands-On Time: 2 minutes**
- **Cook Time: 30 minutes**

Serves 4

1 cup dried pinto beans
4 cups water
1 tablespoon vegetable oil
1 teaspoon salt
1 teaspoon freshly ground
    black pepper

1 Add the beans, water, and oil to the Instant Pot®. Add the salt and pepper, and stir all ingredients until thoroughly combined.

2 Lock the lid into place. Press the Bean button and cook for default time of 30 minutes. (If you prefer beans well done, adjust the cooking time to 40 minutes.)

3 When the timer beeps, let pressure release naturally for 10 minutes. Quick-release any remaining pressure until float valve drops and then unlock lid.

Adzuki Beans

Adzuki (or azuki) beans are an Asian bean that is typically enjoyed sweetened, but they can be served savory too. In Hawaii they are a popular extra in the famous frozen treat known as Shave Ice. These beans are usually a deep, wine-red color, but they also come in white, black, and gray.

- **Hands-On Time: 2 minutes**
- **Cook Time: 30 minutes**

Serves 4

1 cup dried adzuki beans
4 cups water
1 tablespoon vegetable oil
1 teaspoon salt

1 Add the beans, water, and oil to the Instant Pot®. Add the salt, and stir all ingredients until thoroughly combined.

2 Lock the lid into place. Press the Bean button and cook for default time of 30 minutes. (If you prefer beans well done, adjust the cooking time to 40 minutes.)

3 When the timer beeps, let pressure release naturally for 10 minutes. Quick-release any remaining pressure until float valve drops and then unlock lid.

Lima Beans

All beans should be finished using the natural-release method. Lima beans, sometimes called butter beans, contain up to 40 percent of the dietary need for folate, thought to be critical in supporting cellular division and thus in warding off cancer and other illnesses.

- **Hands-On Time: 2 minutes**
- **Cook Time: 30 minutes**

Serves 4

1 cup dried lima beans
4 cups vegetable broth
1 tablespoon vegetable oil

1 Add all ingredients to the Instant Pot® and stir until thoroughly combined.

2 Lock the lid into place. Press the Bean button and cook for default time of 30 minutes. (If you prefer beans well done, adjust the cooking time to 40 minutes.)

3 When timer beeps, let pressure release naturally for 10 minutes. Quick-release any remaining pressure until float valve drops and then unlock lid.

Black Beans

Black beans—a culinary staple in the Americas for at least 7,000 years—are rich in protein, fiber, and omega-3 fatty acids. They're also said to have one of the fastest metabolizing protein speeds and support overall healthy digestion. Adding fat such as vegetable oil to the water while cooking beans will reduce foaming.

- **Hands-On Time: 2 minutes**
- **Cook Time: 30 minutes**

Serves 4

1 cup dried black beans
4 cups water
1 tablespoon vegetable oil
1 teaspoon salt

1 Add the beans, water, and oil to the Instant Pot®. Add the salt, and stir all ingredients until thoroughly combined.

2 Lock the lid into place. Press the Bean button and cook for default time of 30 minutes. (If you prefer beans well done, adjust the cooking time to 40 minutes.)

3 When timer beeps, let pressure release naturally for 10 minutes. Quick-release any remaining pressure until float valve drops and then unlock lid.

Boston-Style Baked Beans

During the Colonial period, the molasses ever-present as a byproduct of Boston's rum trade found its way into many local bean dishes, paving the way for this now-classic dish. They're hearty, savory, and delicious as prepared here, but if you're missing the bacon in these baked beans, try a few pieces of Lightlife Fakin' Bacon.

- **Hands-On Time: 5 minutes**
- **Cook Time: 40 minutes**

Serves 8

2 cups dried navy beans
4 cups water
2 tablespoons vegetable oil
1 teaspoon salt
1 teaspoon liquid smoke
¼ cup diced yellow onion
1 tablespoon prepared yellow mustard
1 tablespoon light brown sugar
1 teaspoon molasses

1 Add the beans, water, oil, salt, and liquid smoke to the Instant Pot®. Stir until thoroughly combined. Lock the lid into place, Press the Bean button, and cook for default time of 30 minutes. (If you prefer beans well done, adjust cooking time to 40 minutes.)

2 When the timer beeps, let pressure release naturally for 10 minutes. Quick-release any remaining pressure until float valve drops and then unlock lid.

3 Press the Sauté button and adjust setting to Less. Add the remaining ingredients and simmer the mixture unlidded 10 minutes to thicken.

White Beans

With so many varietals available—navy, great northern, cannellini, and others all fall under the white bean banner—home cooks are often confused. Don't be. In this and most other recipes, the technique works as described for any and all, and the beans should be chosen according to your preference. Adding a pinch of salt before cooking will help bring out the flavor of the beans.

- **Hands-On Time: 2 minutes**
- **Cook Time: 30 minutes**

Serves 4

1 cup dried cannellini beans
4 cups water
1 tablespoon vegetable oil
1 teaspoon salt

1 Add the beans, water, and oil to the Instant Pot®. Add the salt and stir all ingredients until thoroughly combined.

2 Lock the lid into place. Press the Bean button and cook for default time of 30 minutes. (If you prefer beans well done, adjust the cooking time to 40 minutes.)

3 When the timer beeps, let pressure release naturally for 10 minutes. Quick-release any remaining pressure until float valve drops and then unlock lid.

Lentils

Lentils, a food family of their own and not, as often assumed, a kind of bean, are common in Indian cuisine. They're sometimes underappreciated because they don't can well and are nearly always prepared from scratch. The flavor, texture, and health benefits are well worth your time. Though many cooks do, you needn't soak lentils before cooking.

- **Hands-On Time: 2 minutes**
- **Cook Time: 30 minutes**

Serves 4

1 cup dried lentils (type of choice)
4 cups water
1 tablespoon vegetable oil
1 teaspoon salt

1 Add the lentils, water, and oil to the Instant Pot®. Add the salt and stir all ingredients until thoroughly combined.

2 Lock the lid into place. Press the Bean button and cook for default time of 30 minutes. (If you prefer your lentils well done, adjust cooking time to 40 minutes.)

3 When the timer beeps, let pressure release naturally for 10 minutes. Quick-release any remaining pressure until float valve drops and then unlock lid.

Refried Beans

This Refried Beans dish can be made with black beans instead of the traditional pinto beans. And while the dish is typically served as a side with Mexican meals, a bowl of refried beans, rice, avocado, and faux cheese makes for a quick, high-energy lunch. This dish is especially quick if you start with canned beans, though you'll give up some of the nutrients.

- **Hands-On Time: 10 minutes**
- **Cook Time: 45 minutes**

Serves 8

1 tablespoon olive oil

½ medium yellow onion, peeled and diced

½ small jalapeño pepper, seeded and minced

1 clove garlic, minced

2 cups dried pinto beans

8 cups vegetable broth

½ teaspoon chipotle powder

½ teaspoon ground cumin

1 teaspoon salt

8 ounces vegan Monterey Jack cheese, shredded

MINUS THE LARD

Traditional refried beans are often made with lard, which is not suitable for vegetarians and vegans. To make a vegan version, this recipe calls for olive oil and vegetable broth instead.

1. Press the Sauté button on the Instant Pot® and heat the oil. Add the onion, jalapeño, and garlic; stir-fry 3–5 minutes until onions are translucent.

2. Add the beans, broth, and spices, and stir to combine. Lock the lid into place, press the Bean button, and cook for the default time of 30 minutes.

3. When the timer beeps, let pressure release naturally for 10 minutes. Quick-release any remaining pressure until float valve drops and then unlock lid.

4. Press the Sauté button and adjust temperature to Less. Let simmer while mashing the beans with a masher for 10 minutes until the mixture thickens.

5. Stir in the cheese until thoroughly combined. Serve warm.

Chipotle Thyme Black Beans

There are actually five different varieties of black beans imported into the United States, but we needn't concern ourselves and probably shouldn't, as they are collectively marketed and packaged as "black beans." If, as this recipe suggests, you're starting with dried beans, you may occasionally see the specific varietal name on the bulk bin, but not to worry, any and all will do.

- **Hands-On Time: 2 minutes**
- **Cook Time: 30 minutes**

Serves 8

2 cups dried black beans

5 cups water

1 tablespoon vegetable oil

1 teaspoon chipotle powder

2 teaspoons minced fresh thyme

1 teaspoon salt

1 Add the beans, water, and oil to the Instant Pot®. Add the chipotle powder, thyme, and salt, and stir until thoroughly combined.

2 Lock the lid into place. Press the Bean button and cook for default time of 30 minutes. (If you prefer beans well done, adjust cooking time to 40 minutes.)

3 When the timer beeps, let pressure release naturally for 10 minutes. Quick-release any remaining pressure until float valve drops and then unlock lid.

Beer-Lime Black Beans

Try a Mexican beer such as Negra Modelo, Tecate, or Corona to complement the beans in this recipe. Ginger ale or white grape juice make for passable substitutes if some at your table are avoiding alcohol. Another option: some cooks whip up a blend of vinegar, vegetable broth, and a tablespoon of butter.

- **Hands-On Time: 5 minutes**
- **Cook Time: 35 minutes**

Serves 8

1 tablespoon vegetable oil
½ medium red onion, peeled and diced
1 clove garlic, minced
2 cups dried black beans
3 cups water
2 (12-ounce) bottles light-colored beer, such as a lager or ale
1 tablespoon lime juice
2 teaspoons salt
¼ cup chopped fresh cilantro

1 Press the Sauté button on the Instant Pot® and heat the oil. Add the onion and garlic, and stir-fry 3–5 minutes until onions are translucent.

2 Add the remaining ingredients to the pot and stir to combine. Lock the lid into place, press the Bean button, and cook for the default time of 30 minutes.

3 When the timer beeps, let the pressure release naturally for 10 minutes. Quick-release any remaining pressure until float valve drops and then unlock lid.

4 If a thicker consistency is desired, press the Sauté button and adjust setting to Less; simmer the bean mixture unlidded 10 minutes to thicken.

Chickpea "Tuna" Salad Sandwiches

Chickpeas are also commonly known as garbanzo beans, and are the primary ingredient in hummus. As you'll find with this recipe, given a little time in the Instant Pot®, they also make a fantastic tuna salad substitute.

- **Hands-On Time: 10 minutes**
- **Cook Time: 30 minutes**

Serves 4

1 cup dried chickpeas

5 cups water

6" piece dried kombu

1 tablespoon vegetable oil

2 tablespoons sweet relish

½ medium stalk celery, minced

¼ medium red onion, peeled and minced

¼ cup vegan mayonnaise

1 teaspoon fresh lemon juice

½ teaspoon dried dill

1 teaspoon salt

4 vegan sandwich buns

4 lettuce leaves (optional)

4 slices tomato (optional)

KOMBU

Kombu is a type of edible seaweed that is typically sold in sheets. It is often used to flavor soups and other savory dishes because it adds the umami flavor.

1 Add the chickpeas, water, kombu, and oil to the Instant Pot®. Stir ingredients until thoroughly combined.

2 Lock the lid into place. Press the Bean button and cook for default time of 30 minutes.

3 When the timer beeps, let pressure release naturally for 10 minutes. Quick-release any remaining pressure until float valve drops and then unlock lid.

4 Transfer the chickpeas to a large bowl and mash.

5 Add the relish, celery, onion, mayonnaise, lemon juice, dill, and salt, and stir until well combined. Scoop into a small dish, cover, and refrigerate 1–2 hours.

6 Divide the mixture evenly over the 4 sandwich buns, top with lettuce and tomato if desired, and serve.

New Orleans Red Beans and Rice

New Orleans Red Beans and Rice is a staple now eaten every day across the bayou country, but it was traditionally eaten primarily on Mondays. According to folklore, this was because Monday was reserved for laundry in old Louisiana, and cooks would soak their red beans while the clothing dried.

- **Hands-On Time: 5 minutes**
- **Cook Time: 35 minutes**

Serves 8

3 tablespoons vegan margarine

1 cup diced white onion

1 cup diced green bell pepper

1 cup diced celery

2 cloves garlic, minced

2¼ cups dried red kidney beans

5 cups vegetable broth

1 teaspoon liquid smoke

½ teaspoon vegan Worcestershire sauce

1 teaspoon hot sauce (or more if desired)

½ teaspoon dried thyme

1 teaspoon cayenne pepper

2 bay leaves

2 teaspoons salt

8 cups cooked long-grain white rice

1 Press the Sauté button on the Instant Pot®. Heat the margarine, then add the onions, bell pepper, celery, and garlic. Stir fry 3–5 minutes or until onions are translucent.

2 Add the beans, broth, liquid smoke, Worcestershire, hot sauce, thyme, cayenne, bay leaves, and salt, and stir to combine. Lock the lid into place, press the Bean button, and cook for the default time of 30 minutes.

3 When the timer beeps, let the pressure release naturally for 10 minutes. Quick-release any remaining pressure until float valve drops and then unlock lid.

4 If a thicker consistency is desired, press the Sauté button and adjust setting to Less; simmer the bean mixture unlidded 10 minutes to thicken.

5 Remove the bay leaves before serving and season with additional salt and hot sauce to taste. Serve over cooked rice.

MAKE IT "MEATY"

To make a vegan "meaty" version of this dish, add cooked, sliced vegan sausage and chunks of cooked vegan bacon right before serving.

Red Beans with Plantains

Red Beans with Plantains is a common dish in Ghana and in parts of the Caribbean. As with many other bean dishes, this recipe seems to run a bit long for something you're making in the Instant Pot®. Often this time can be greatly reduced by simply opting for canned, precooked beans—in this case, though, starting from dried red beans is highly recommended.

- **Hands-On Time: 15 minutes**
- **Cook Time: 45 minutes**

Serves 8

1 cup canola oil

3 ripened plantains, peeled and sliced diagonally

4 tablespoons olive oil, divided

1 cup diced red onion

4 cloves garlic, minced

1 teaspoon peeled and minced fresh ginger

2 teaspoons salt, plus more to taste

½ teaspoon cayenne pepper

1 cup diced tomatoes

Pinch freshly ground black pepper

2 cups dried red beans

5 cups water

1 Press the Sauté button on the Instant Pot® and add the canola oil. Add the plantains and stir-fry 5–7 minutes or until slightly crispy. Remove plantains from Instant Pot® and set aside.

2 Add 2 tablespoons olive oil and sauté the onions 2–3 minutes or until translucent. Add the garlic, ginger, salt, and cayenne and sauté 1 minute more. Add the tomatoes and pepper, and bring to a simmer 2–3 minutes. Add the beans, water, and remaining oil.

3 Lock the lid into place, press the Bean button, and cook for the default time of 30 minutes.

4 When the timer beeps, let the pressure release naturally for 10 minutes. Quick-release any remaining pressure until float valve drops and then unlock lid.

5 If a thicker consistency is desired, press the Sauté button and adjust setting to Less; simmer the bean mixture unlidded 10 minutes to thicken.

6 Transfer bean mixture to bowls and top with plantains. Taste for seasoning and add more salt if desired.

White Beans and Rice

Odd though it may sound as a condiment here, a touch of yellow mustard finishes off this dish surprisingly well. White Beans and Rice emerges from the widely revered culinary culture of southern Louisiana, where it is often prepared very much as described here, and sometimes with a bit of spinach.

- **Hands-On Time: 5 minutes**
- **Cook Time: 35 minutes**

Serves 8

3 tablespoons canola oil, divided

1 cup diced white onion

1 medium green bell pepper, seeded and chopped

1 medium stalk celery, chopped

3 cloves garlic, minced

2 cups dried white northern beans

6 cups water

¼ teaspoon cayenne pepper

2 bay leaves

Pinch salt

Pinch freshly ground black pepper

4 cups cooked long-grain white rice

1 Press the Sauté button on the Instant Pot®. Heat 2 tablespoons oil and sauté the onions, bell pepper, celery, and garlic 4–5 minutes or until onions are translucent and mixture is fragrant and slightly browned.

2 Add the beans, water, cayenne, and bay leaves, and stir to combine thoroughly. Lock the lid into place, press the Bean button, and cook for the default time of 30 minutes.

3 When the timer beeps, let the pressure release naturally for 10 minutes. Quick-release any remaining pressure until float valve drops and then unlock lid.

4 Remove the bay leaves. If a thicker consistency is desired, press the Sauté button and adjust button setting to Less; simmer the bean mixture unlidded 10 minutes to thicken.

5 Season with salt and pepper. Serve over the cooked white rice.

FLAVOR VARIATIONS

Give this dish Italian flair by adding chopped tomatoes, fresh basil, and chopped and pitted olives.

Hoppin' John

Also known as Carolina Peas and Rice, Hoppin' John is a New Year's Day tradition in the southern United States. The dish's simplicity is said to speak to the eater's frugality and pennywise ways which, it is hoped, will bring good fortune in the new year.

- **Hands-On Time: 5 minutes**
- **Cook Time: 35 minutes**

Serves 4

1 tablespoon olive oil
½ cup yellow diced onion
1 clove garlic, minced
1 cup dried black-eyed peas
4 cups vegetable broth
1 bay leaf
1 teaspoon chipotle powder
1 teaspoon salt
2 cups cooked long-grain
   white rice

1 Press the Sauté button on the Instant Pot® and add the oil. Add the onion and sauté 3 minutes. Add the garlic and sauté an additional 30 seconds.

2 Add the peas, broth, bay leaf, chipotle powder, and salt to the pot. Lock the lid into place, press the Bean button, and cook for the default time of 30 minutes. When the timer beeps, quick-release pressure until float valve drops, then unlock lid.

3 Remove bay leaf. Stir in the rice and serve.

Lentil-Spinach Curry

Like so many other once-exotic foods and spices, curry powder can now be found in almost any grocery store. You are sacrificing a bit on quality unless you're getting relatively fresh powder, so make a point to seek out an Asian or South Asian grocer near you. Any such market will likely offer several varieties, any of which will work in this recipe.

- **Hands-On Time: 5 minutes**
- **Cook Time: 35 minutes**

Serves 4

2 tablespoons olive oil, divided
½ cup diced Vidalia onion
1 clove garlic, minced
½ teaspoon ground coriander
½ teaspoon turmeric powder
½ teaspoon curry powder
1 cup yellow lentils
4 cups water
½ cup diced tomato
2 cups fresh spinach leaves

1 Press the Sauté button on the Instant Pot®. Heat 1 tablespoon oil and sauté the onions 2–3 minutes or until translucent. Add the garlic, coriander, turmeric, and curry powder, and sauté additional 30 seconds.

2 Add the lentils, water, and remaining oil to the pot, and stir to combine thoroughly. Lock the lid into place, press the Bean button, and cook for the default time of 30 minutes.

3 When the timer beeps, let pressure release naturally for 10 minutes. Quick-release any remaining pressure until float valve drops and then unlock lid.

4 Remove the lid and stir in tomatoes and spinach. Stir to combine thoroughly until spinach is wilted, about 1 minute.

Red Lentil Curry

Red lentils, very common in North African and Middle Eastern cooking, have a distinctive flavor and, with their rich, deep color, make for a gorgeous presentation on the plate. You can simplify the seasoning in Red Lentil Curry by omitting the turmeric and ginger.

- **Hands-On Time: 10 minutes**
- **Cook Time: 40 minutes**

Serves 8

3 tablespoons olive oil, divided
1 cup diced yellow onion
1 teaspoon minced garlic
1 teaspoon minced fresh ginger
3 tablespoons curry powder
1 teaspoon turmeric powder
1 teaspoon ground cumin
1 teaspoon chili powder
1 teaspoon granulated sugar
1 (6-ounce) can tomato paste
2 cups dried red lentils
8 cups water
1 teaspoon salt, plus more to taste
Pinch freshly ground black pepper

1 Press the Sauté button on the Instant Pot®. Heat 2 tablespoons oil and sauté the onions 4–5 minutes or until caramelized. Add the garlic and ginger, and sauté 1 minute. Add the curry powder, turmeric, cumin, chili powder, sugar, and tomato paste, and bring the mixture to a simmer 2–3 minutes, stirring constantly. Transfer the mixture to a bowl and set aside.

2 Add the lentils, water, and remaining oil to the pot, and stir to combine thoroughly. Lock the lid into place, press the Bean button, and cook for the default time of 30 minutes.

3 When the timer beeps, let the pressure release naturally for 10 minutes. Quick-release any remaining pressure until float valve drops and then unlock lid.

4 Remove the lid, add the sautéed onion mixture, season with salt and pepper, and stir to combine thoroughly.

Edamame-Seaweed Salad

Edamame is an increasingly popular salted soybean dish that, like seaweed, arrived in American cuisine from Japan and other Asia-Pacific nations. Many Americans first tasted seaweed as a sushi wrapper and have more recently ventured toward other preparations. There are many types of edible seaweed, the most popular varieties of late including nori, arame, hijiki, and wakame.

- **Hands-On Time: 5 minutes**
- **Cook Time: 20 minutes**

Serves 4

1 tablespoon sesame oil
1 clove garlic, minced
½ teaspoon minced fresh
   ginger
1 cup shelled edamame
4 cups water
1 tablespoon vegetable oil
½ cup chopped dried arame
1 teaspoon rice wine vinegar
1 teaspoon salt

1 Press the Sauté button on the Instant Pot®. Heat the sesame oil and sauté the garlic and ginger 1–2 minutes. Remove from the pot and set aside.

2 Add the edamame, water, and vegetable oil to the pot, and stir to combine thoroughly. Lock the lid into place and press the Bean button. Adjust timer to 25 minutes.

3 While the edamame is cooking, cover the arame with water in a small bowl and let sit 7 minutes. Drain and set aside.

4 When the timer beeps, let pressure release naturally for 10 minutes. Quick-release any remaining pressure until float valve drops and then unlock lid.

5 Stir in sautéed garlic and ginger, vinegar, salt, and arame. Serve warm or chilled.

Dinner Loaf

Meatloaf lovers who've committed to a vegan diet often find it's one of those dishes that can be very tough to prepare to vegan standards. Instant Pot® Dinner Loaf to the rescue! Especially when you start with dried pinto beans, this dish is packed with healthful flavors. In fact, the ingredients and preparation are very similar to those found in gallo pinto, a Nicaraguan staple.

- **Hands-On Time: 10 minutes**
- **Cook Time: 65 minutes**

Serves 6

1 cup dried pinto beans
4 cups water
1 tablespoon vegetable oil
1 teaspoon salt
1 cup diced yellow onion
1 cup chopped walnuts
½ cup rolled oats
1 teaspoon cornstarch
   combined with
   1 tablespoon water
¾ cup ketchup
1 teaspoon garlic powder
1 teaspoon dried basil
1 teaspoon dried parsley
Pinch salt
Pinch freshly ground black
   pepper

1   Heat the oven to 350°F. Spray a 9" × 5" loaf pan with cooking spray.

2   Add the beans, water, oil, and salt to the Instant Pot® and stir to combine thoroughly. Lock the lid into place, press the Bean button, and cook for the default time of 30 minutes.

3   When the timer beeps, let pressure release naturally for 10 minutes. Quick-release any remaining pressure until float valve drops and then unlock lid.

4   Transfer the beans to a large mixing bowl and add the remaining ingredients; mix well.

5   Spread the mixture into the prepared loaf pan and bake 30–35 minutes.

MOCK MEATLOAF

There are many ingredients you can use to make mock meatloaf. For the easiest option, use vegan ground beef, such as Gimme Lean Ground Beef Style, instead of real meat in your favorite recipe.

8

Tofu, Seitan, and Tempeh

Tofu is probably one of the most-consumed proteins for vegans, and the "wheat-meat" of seitan is not far behind. There are a million recipes and a handful of go-to meals that you can cook for your family. But if you're sick of eating the same old things week after week, the Instant Pot® is your new best friend. The steam and pressure used to cook items in the pot are guaranteed to leave the dishes in this chapter juicy and delicious! Whether you're craving Barbecue Tofu Sandwiches, Lemon Tofu Tacos, Seitan Sloppy Joes, or Smoked Portobello and Seitan, you'll find a new favorite recipe here!

Marinated Tofu Steaks

Tofu has little flavor on its own and is often marinated in a flavorful liquid before cooking, as here in a soy-vinegar mixture. It's always a good idea and you are encouraged, especially with tofu dishes, to get a bit of practice before putting it on a menu for guests, as the consistency and texture will vary with only slight alterations in preparation and timing.

- **Hands-On Time: 5 minutes**
- **Cook Time: 10 minutes**

Serves 2

16 ounces extra-firm tofu

1 cup soy sauce

1 tablespoon white wine vinegar

1 teaspoon minced garlic

1 teaspoon minced fresh ginger

2 tablespoons vegetable oil

1 cup water

1 Drain the tofu, pat dry with a towel or paper towel, and then cut into 4 equal-sized pieces. Place in a 1"-deep dish.

2 In a medium bowl, whisk together the soy sauce, vinegar, garlic, and ginger, and then pour over the tofu. Let stand 10 minutes, being sure to turn the tofu often or spoon the excess liquid over the top.

3 Press the Sauté button on the Instant Pot® and add the oil. Add the tofu steaks and sauté until brown on each side, about 3 minutes per side. Remove the tofu steaks.

4 Pour the water into the pot and insert the steamer tray. Place the tofu steaks on top of the steamer tray. Lock the lid into place, press the Steam button, and adjust timer to 5 minutes. When the timer beeps, let pressure release naturally until float valve drops and then unlock lid. Serve immediately.

Barbecue Tofu Sandwiches

Many breads are vegan, to be sure, but by no means all of them. Be sure to read the label on your hamburger buns to ensure you're on the safe side. If buying fresh from a baker, it's always better to ask than to assume.

- **Hands-On Time: 10 minutes**
- **Cook Time: 7 minutes**

Serves 6

16 ounces firm tofu
1 teaspoon dried mustard
¼ cup light brown sugar
¾ cup apple cider vinegar
¼ cup water
2 tablespoons chili powder
½ teaspoon soy sauce
¼ teaspoon cayenne pepper
2 tablespoons vegan margarine
1 tablespoon liquid smoke
Pinch salt
Pinch freshly ground black pepper
6 hamburger buns

1 Wrap the block of tofu in paper towels and press 5 minutes by adding a heavy plate on top.

2 Whisk together all ingredients except tofu and buns in a medium bowl.

3 Crumble the tofu with your hands and mix it into the barbecue sauce mixture. Pour the barbecue tofu mixture into the Instant Pot®. Lock the lid into place, press the Manual button, and adjust timer to 7 minutes.

4 When the timer beeps, let pressure release naturally until float valve drops and then unlock lid. Serve on hamburger buns.

Lemon Tofu Tacos

Tofu mimics the role of fish in these easy-to-make tacos, but does tend to lack the flavor of all but the wateriest whitefish. A simple solution: kick up the flavor by adding a touch of cayenne or chipotle pepper to the tofu marinade, or just to half of it, which sets up nicely to serve these tacos to the adventurous and spice-averse alike.

- **Hands-On Time: 2 minutes**
- **Cook Time: 10 minutes**

Serves 4

16 ounces extra-firm tofu
2 tablespoons lemon juice
½ tablespoon apple cider vinegar
2 tablespoons soy sauce
2 tablespoons olive oil
1 cup water
8 (6") corn tortillas, warmed
1 medium tomato, diced
½ medium red onion, peeled and thinly sliced
2 teaspoons chopped fresh cilantro
Pinch salt
Pinch freshly ground black pepper

CORN VERSUS FLOUR TORTILLAS

There is no right or wrong answer as to which is better. It solely depends on your taste. Corn tortillas are more full-flavored than flour and they also have a grainier texture. Which variety you decide to use is up to you!

1 Wrap the block of tofu in paper towels and press for 5 minutes by adding a heavy plate on top. Remove the paper towels and cut the tofu into ½"-thick pieces. Place in a 1"-deep dish.

2 Whisk together the lemon juice, vinegar, soy sauce, and olive oil in a small bowl and pour it over the tofu. Let stand 10 minutes, being sure to turn the tofu often or spoon the excess liquid over the top.

3 Set the steamer tray inside the Instant Pot® and place the marinated tofu on top of the steamer tray. Pour the water into the pot and press the Steam button. Adjust timer to 5 minutes. When the timer beeps, let pressure release naturally until float valve drops and then unlock lid.

4 Place the tofu on the tortillas and top each with equal amounts tomato, onion, and cilantro. Season with salt and pepper. Serve immediately.

Blackened Tofu

Preparing blackened tofu on the grill is a delicious way to give your Instant Pot® a quick break on a warm summer day. On the other hand, at 15 minutes from start to finish, why not? The apple cider and garlic flavors are delicious when sautéed together, making this great for your next afternoon gathering.

- **Hands-On Time: 5 minutes**
- **Cook Time: 10 minutes**

Serves 6

16 ounces extra-firm tofu
⅓ cup soy sauce
1 tablespoon apple cider vinegar
1 tablespoon minced garlic
1 tablespoon paprika
2 teaspoons freshly ground black pepper
1½ teaspoons salt
1 teaspoon garlic powder
1 teaspoon cayenne pepper
½ teaspoon dried oregano
½ teaspoon dried thyme
2 tablespoons vegetable oil
1 cup water

1 Drain the tofu, press dry with a towel or paper towel, and then cut into four equal-sized pieces. Place in a 1"-deep dish.

2 In a small bowl whisk together the soy sauce, vinegar, and garlic, and then pour over the tofu. Let stand 10 minutes, being sure to turn the tofu often or spoon the excess liquid over the top.

3 To make the blackened seasoning mixture, combine the paprika, pepper, salt, garlic powder, cayenne, oregano, and thyme in a small bowl. Remove the tofu from the soy marinade and dip each side into the seasoning.

4 Add the oil to the Instant Pot® and press the Sauté button. Sauté the blackened tofu until brown on each side, about 3 minutes per side. Remove the blackened tofu.

5 Pour the water into the pot and set the steamer tray inside. Place the blackened tofu on top of the steamer tray. Lock the lid into place, press the Steam button, and adjust time to 5 minutes. When the timer beeps, let pressure release naturally until float valve drops and then unlock lid. Serve immediately.

Coconut Green Curry Tofu

Coconut milk can range from thin and watery to the near-solid consumed as candy throughout the Pacific. Experiment with different types of coconut milk until you find the one you like best. Or get really adventurous, find some coconuts at an Asian market near you, and learn to "milk" them yourself!

- **Hands-On Time: 5 minutes**
- **Cook Time: 10 minutes**

Serves 4

16 ounces extra-firm tofu

2 medium green chilies, seeded and minced

4 green onions, chopped

2 cloves garlic, minced

1 teaspoon minced fresh ginger

1 tablespoon soy sauce

½ cup chopped fresh cilantro

¼ cup chopped fresh Italian flat-leaf parsley

2 tablespoons water

2 tablespoons vegetable oil

1 (13.5-ounce) can coconut milk

Pinch salt

Pinch freshly ground black pepper

4 cups cooked brown rice

1 Wrap the block of tofu in paper towels and press 5 minutes by placing a heavy plate on top. Remove the paper towels and cut the tofu into ½"-thick pieces.

2 In a food processor, combine the chilies, green onions, garlic, ginger, soy sauce, cilantro, parsley, and water. Blend into a smooth paste, adding extra water if necessary.

3 Press the Sauté button on the Instant Pot® and add the oil. Sauté the tofu until it is lightly browned on all sides, about 3 minutes per side.

4 Add the coconut milk and green chili paste to the pot. Lock the lid into place, press the Manual button, and adjust timer to 5 minutes. When the timer beeps, let pressure release naturally until float valve drops and then unlock lid.

5 Season with salt and pepper. Serve with rice.

Panang Curry Tofu

Panang is a mild type of red curry and is distinguished from other red curries largely by the chilies and thick coconut milk with which it is made. Contrary to the assumptions Americans sometimes make about the cuisine of "the old world," panang curry didn't make its first appearance in the written record of Siamese/Thai cuisine until just over a century ago, in 1890.

- **Hands-On Time: 10 minutes**
- **Cook Time: 12 minutes**

Serves 4

16 ounces extra-firm tofu

1 (13.5-ounce) can coconut milk

1 tablespoon panang curry paste

2 tablespoons soy sauce

1 tablespoon lime juice

2 tablespoons granulated sugar

2 tablespoons olive oil

¼ medium sweet onion, peeled and sliced

½ medium carrot, peeled and sliced diagonally

¼ medium red bell pepper, seeded and chopped

½ cup chopped fresh basil

4 cups basmati cooked rice

1. Wrap the block of tofu in paper towels and press 5 minutes by adding a heavy plate on top. Remove the paper towels and cut the tofu into ½"-thick pieces. Place in a 1"-deep dish.

2. In a medium bowl combine the coconut milk, curry paste, soy sauce, lime juice, and sugar.

3. Press the Sauté button on the Instant Pot® and add the oil. Add the tofu and sauté until lightly browned on all sides, about 3 minutes. Add the onion, carrot, and bell pepper; sauté 1–2 minutes more.

4. Add the curry sauce to the pot. Lock the lid into place, press the Manual button, and adjust timer to 5 minutes. When the timer beeps, let pressure release naturally until float valve drops and then unlock lid.

5. Garnish the tofu with fresh basil. Serve with rice.

Tofu Stir-Fry with Vegetables

Unless you own a wok you'll likely find this the closest you've ever come to the texture and temperature of restaurant vegetable stir-fries, as the Instant Pot® allows for a very similar quick-sauté approach.

- **Hands-On Time: 10 minutes**
- **Cook Time: 10 minutes**

Serves 2

16 ounces extra-firm tofu

1 medium red chili pepper, seeded and minced

2 cloves garlic, minced

1 teaspoon minced fresh ginger

1 tablespoon olive oil

3 tablespoons soy sauce

¼ cup water

1 tablespoon cornstarch

2 tablespoons vegetable oil

2 medium carrots, peeled and cut diagonally

1 medium red bell pepper, seeded and chopped

½ medium sweet onion, peeled and sliced

2 cups chopped bok choy

½ cup chopped yellow squash

4 cups cooked long-grain white rice

1 Wrap the block of tofu in paper towels and press 5 minutes by adding a heavy plate on top. Remove the paper towels and cut the tofu into ½"-thick pieces. Place in a 1"-deep dish.

2 In a medium bowl, combine the chili pepper, garlic, ginger, olive oil, soy sauce, water, and cornstarch. Pour it over the tofu. Let stand 10 minutes, being sure to turn the tofu often or spoon the excess liquid over the top. Reserve the excess marinade.

3 Press the Sauté button on the Instant Pot® and add the vegetable oil. Sauté the tofu until light brown on all sides, about 3 minutes per side. Add the carrot, bell pepper, onion, bok choy, and yellow squash; sauté 1–2 minutes.

4 Pour the reserved marinade into the pot. Lock the lid into place, press the Manual Button, and adjust timer to 5 minutes. When the timer beeps, let pressure release naturally until float valve drops and then unlock lid.

5 Serve the stir-fry with the cooked rice.

COOKING WITH CORNSTARCH
To help thicken a sauce or stew, use cornstarch. To avoid lumps, combine cornstarch with a small amount of cold water, stir until dissolved, then slowly add it to your dish, stirring over low heat until thickened.

General Tso's Tofu

The combination of sweet and spicy is what makes General Tso's Tofu a hit at Chinese restaurants across the country and around the world. Traditional wok-based dishes make for great Instant Pot® conversions as the cooking intensity calls to mind a bit what is called the "breath of the wok."

- **Hands-On Time: 5 minutes**
- **Cook Time: 10 minutes**

Serves 2

16 ounces extra-firm tofu
1 cup water
2 tablespoons cornstarch
2 cloves garlic, minced
1 teaspoon minced fresh ginger
⅛ cup granulated sugar
¼ cup soy sauce
⅛ cup white wine vinegar
⅛ cup sherry wine
2 teaspoons cayenne pepper
2 tablespoons vegetable oil
2 cups chopped broccoli, blanched
4 cups cooked long-grain white rice

1 Wrap the block of tofu in paper towels and press 5 minutes by adding weight on top. Remove the paper towels and cut the tofu into ½"-thick pieces.

2 In a small bowl, whisk together water, cornstarch, garlic, ginger, sugar, soy sauce, vinegar, wine, and cayenne pepper. Set this General Tso's sauce aside.

3 Press the Sauté button on the Instant Pot® and add the oil. Add the tofu and sauté until brown on all sides. Add the broccoli and sauté 1 minute more.

4 Add the General Tso's sauce to the pot. Lock the lid into place, press the Manual button, and adjust timer to 5 minutes. When the timer beeps, quick-release pressure until float valve drops and then unlock lid. Serve with cooked rice.

TYPES OF RICE
Options are diverse when choosing a rice or grain to serve with a Chinese or Chinese-inspired tofu dish. Long-grain white rice is most commonly used, but you can also use brown rice, quinoa, or couscous. See Chapter 6 for recipes and cooking times.

Kung Pao Tofu

Kung Pao Chicken is a traditional Szechuan dish that can easily be made vegan by replacing the chicken with extra-firm tofu. Emphasis on "extra-firm" here—softer varieties of tofu require an extremely delicate touch to survive the high temperatures and pressures this dish requires, in the Instant Pot® and otherwise.

- **Hands-On Time: 10 minutes**
- **Cook Time: 11 minutes**

Serves 2

16 ounces extra-firm tofu
2 tablespoons dry white wine
2 tablespoons soy sauce
2 tablespoons sesame oil
2 tablespoons cornstarch, dissolved in 2 tablespoons water
½ tablespoon hot chili paste
1 teaspoon rice wine vinegar
2 teaspoons light brown sugar
1 cup water
1 teaspoon olive oil
½ medium red bell pepper, seeded and chopped
1 clove garlic, minced
¼ cup chopped peanuts
4 cups cooked long-grain white rice

1 Wrap the block of tofu in paper towels and press 5 minutes by adding a heavy plate on top. Remove the paper towels and cut the tofu into ½"-thick pieces. Place in a 1"-deep dish.

2 In a small bowl, whisk together the wine, soy sauce, sesame oil, cornstarch mixture, chili paste, vinegar, and sugar. Pour it over the tofu. Let stand 10 minutes, being sure to turn the tofu often or spoon the excess liquid over the top.

3 Pour the water into the Instant Pot® and insert the steamer tray. Place the marinated tofu on top of the steamer tray. Press the Steam button on the pot and adjust the timer to 5 minutes. Remove the tofu and steamer tray.

4 Press the Sauté button and add the oil to the pot. Sauté the bell pepper 1–2 minutes. Add the marinated tofu and garlic and sauté 1 minute more. Add the sauce and cook 2–3 minutes more. Toss mixture with the peanuts and serve with rice.

Palak Tofu Paneer

The original Indian paneer is a type of cheese, but for our purposes we can use tofu instead. Much of the flavor in this and other paneer dishes comes from the cumin and coriander, so some taste buds may prefer a slightly larger portion of these herbs than the ones listed here.

- **Hands-On Time: 5 minutes**
- **Cook Time: 10 minutes**

Serves 2

16 ounces extra-firm tofu
2 tablespoons vegetable oil
2 cloves garlic, minced
1 teaspoon minced fresh ginger
2 teaspoons dried red pepper flakes
½ medium yellow onion, peeled and diced
1 tablespoon ground cumin
1 teaspoon ground coriander
1 teaspoon granulated sugar
1 teaspoon turmeric powder
1 cup soy sour cream
6 cups fresh spinach leaves
⅛ cup chopped fresh cilantro
Pinch salt
Pinch freshly ground black pepper
2 cups cooked brown rice

1 Wrap the block of tofu in paper towels and press 5 minutes by adding a heavy plate on top. Remove the paper towels and cut the tofu into ½"-thick pieces.

2 Press the Sauté button on the Instant Pot® and add the oil. Sauté the tofu until lightly browned on all sides. Add the garlic, ginger, red pepper flakes, onion, cumin, coriander, sugar, and turmeric. Sauté 1–2 minutes more.

3 Mix in the sour cream and spinach and stir continuously 2–3 more minutes or until spinach is wilted and all ingredients are thoroughly combined.

4 Garnish with cilantro and add salt and pepper. Serve with rice.

Homemade Seitan

When pressed for time, use packaged seitan instead of making it at home, but we recommend giving this recipe a try. Seitan is a popular vegan protein but still a bit mysterious to many cooks—you'll find that the Instant Pot® makes the process surprisingly simple.

- **Hands-On Time: 25 minutes**
- **Cook Time: 20 minutes**

Yields 1¼ pounds

3½ cups whole-wheat flour
3½ cups unbleached white flour
3½ cups cold water, as needed
7 cups vegetable broth

SEITAN VARIATIONS

The taste and texture of seitan can vary greatly depending on the type of flour you use and the amount of time spent kneading the dough. Experiment with different combinations until you reach the consistency most pleasing to your palate.

1 Place the whole-wheat and unbleached flour in a large mixing bowl and stir well to combine. While stirring, gradually pour enough water into the flour to form a sticky dough that can be kneaded (amount of water needed may vary due to humidity, etc.). Knead 15 minutes. Cover the dough with remaining water, place in the refrigerator, and keep submerged at least 30 minutes.

2 Transfer the dough to a colander and place it in the sink. Under cold running water, carefully knead the dough, rinsing out the starch and bran. After several minutes of cold-water rinsing and kneading, the gluten will start to stick together. Alternate between room-temperature water and cold-water rinses while continuing to knead the dough until it has a firm, rubbery texture.

3 Add the broth to the Instant Pot®. Tear off pieces of the dough and roll into 1" balls (about the size of Ping-Pong balls). Drop the balls of dough into the liquid one at a time, stirring occasionally to prevent sticking. Lock the lid into place, press the Manual button, and adjust timer to 20 minutes. When the timer beeps, quick-release pressure until float valve drops and then unlock lid.

4 The seitan can be refrigerated in the cooking liquid 3–4 days.

Seitan Sloppy Joes

Said to have emerged in Sioux City, Iowa, in the early twentieth century, the Sloppy Joe is an American summer standby. Add to the deliciously messy madness by tossing vegan cheese and diced onions onto this delicious sandwich. Be sure to have extra napkins on hand!

- **Hands-On Time: 25 minutes**
- **Cook Time: 28 minutes**

Serves 4

1¾ cups whole-wheat flour

1¾ cups unbleached white flour

1¾ cups cold water, as needed

3½ cups vegetable broth

1 tablespoon olive oil

½ medium yellow onion, peeled and diced

½ teaspoon garlic powder

2 teaspoons light brown sugar

1 tablespoon prepared yellow mustard

¾ cup ketchup

1 tablespoon vegan Worcestershire sauce

Pinch salt

Pinch freshly ground black pepper

6–8 vegan hamburger buns

SEITAN ALTERNATIVES

There are many alternatives to homemade seitan when making sloppy joes. Crumbled tofu or tempeh will work, as well as vegan beef substitutes, such as Boca Veggie Ground Crumbles.

1 Place the whole-wheat and unbleached flour in a large mixing bowl and stir well to combine. While stirring, gradually pour enough water into the flour to form a sticky dough that can be kneaded. Knead 15 minutes. Cover the dough with cold water, place in the refrigerator, and keep submerged at least 30 minutes.

2 Transfer the dough to a colander and place it in the sink. Under cold running water, carefully knead the dough, rinsing out the starch and bran. After several minutes of cold-water rinsing and kneading, the gluten will start to stick together. Alternate between room-temperature water and cold-water rinses while continuing to knead the dough until it has a firm, rubbery texture.

3 Pour the broth into the Instant Pot®. Tear apart pieces of the dough and form into 1" balls (about the size of Ping-Pong balls). Drop the balls of dough into the broth one piece at a time, stirring occasionally to prevent sticking.

4 Lock the lid into place. Press the Manual button and adjust the timer to 20 minutes. When the timer beeps, quick-release pressure until float valve drops and then unlock lid. Remove the seitan and drain the remaining liquid from the pot. Slice the seitan very thinly.

5 Press the Sauté button on the pot and add the oil. Sauté the onion until it turns golden brown. Add the seitan and the rest of the ingredients except buns. Let simmer 5–8 minutes. Serve on hamburger buns.

Shredded BBQ Seitan

Bottled barbecue sauce will work just as well as the do-it-yourself option mentioned in Step 5 of this recipe; as always, if you do opt for store-bought just make sure it's vegan.

- **Hands-On Time: 25 minutes**
- **Cook Time: 27 minutes**

Serves 4

1¾ cups whole-wheat flour

1¾ cups unbleached white flour

1¾ cups cold water, as needed

3½ cups vegetable broth

1 cup prepared yellow mustard

½ cup granulated sugar

¼ cup light brown sugar

¾ cup apple cider vinegar

2 tablespoons chili powder

¼ tablespoon cayenne pepper

1 teaspoon soy sauce

2 tablespoons vegan margarine

1 tablespoon liquid smoke

Pinch salt

Pinch freshly ground black pepper

1. Place the whole-wheat and unbleached flour in a large mixing bowl and stir well to combine. While stirring, gradually pour enough water into the flour to form a sticky dough that can be kneaded. Knead 15 minutes. Cover the dough with cold water and place in the refrigerator at least 30 minutes.

2. Transfer the dough to a colander and place it in the sink. Under cold running water, carefully knead the dough, rinsing out the starch and bran. After several minutes the gluten will start to stick together. Alternate between room-temperature water and cold-water rinses while continuing to knead the dough until it has a firm, rubbery texture.

3. Pour the broth into the Instant Pot®. Tear pieces of the dough and form into 1" balls (about the size of Ping-Pong balls). Drop the dough into the liquid one piece at a time, stirring occasionally to prevent sticking.

4. Lock the lid into place. Press the Manual button and adjust the timer to 20 minutes. When the timer beeps, quick-release pressure until float valve drops and then unlock lid. Remove the seitan, and drain the liquid.

5. Press the Sauté button on the pot and adjust to Low. Add the mustard, sugars, vinegar, chili powder, cayenne pepper, soy sauce, vegan margarine, liquid smoke, salt, and pepper to the pot, and stir constantly.

6. Shred the seitan by hand or with a knife and add to the prepared barbecue sauce. Let simmer about 5–7 minutes. Serve.

Seitan with Sauerkraut and Onions

An ale, or another light beer, is recommended over dark beers in this recipe as the thicker brews tend to overwhelm the rest of the flavors by the time they emerge from the Instant Pot®. If you prefer not to use beer at all, try white grape juice or ginger ale.

- **Hands-On Time: 25 minutes**
- **Cook Time: 30 minutes**

Serves 4

1¾ cups whole-wheat flour

1¾ cups unbleached white flour

1¾ cups cold water, as needed

3½ cups vegetable broth

¼ cup olive oil

3 medium yellow onions, peeled and thinly sliced

2 teaspoons light brown sugar

3 cups sauerkraut

2 cloves garlic, minced

2 bay leaves

4 red potatoes, peeled and quartered

2 medium carrots, peeled and roughly chopped

1 (12-ounce) beer of your choice

Pinch salt

Pinch freshly ground black pepper

½ cup chopped fresh Italian flat-leaf parsley (optional)

1 Place the whole-wheat and unbleached flour in a large mixing bowl and stir well to combine. While stirring, gradually pour enough water into the flour to form a sticky dough that can be kneaded. Knead 15 minutes. Cover the dough with cold water and place in the refrigerator at least 30 minutes.

2 Transfer the dough to a colander and place it in the sink. Under cold running water, carefully knead the dough, rinsing out the starch and bran. After several minutes of cold-water rinsing and kneading, the gluten will start to stick together. Alternate between room-temperature water and cold-water rinses while continuing to knead the dough until it has a firm, rubbery texture.

3 Pour the broth into the Instant Pot®. Tear apart pieces of the dough and form into 1" balls (about the size of Ping-Pong balls). Drop the balls of dough into the liquid one at a time, stirring occasionally to prevent sticking.

4 Lock the lid into place, press the Manual button, and adjust the timer to 20 minutes. When the timer beeps, quick-release the pressure until float valve drops and then unlock lid. Remove the seitan and chop into bite-sized pieces. Drain the liquid from the pot.

5 Return the seitan to the pot and add all remaining ingredients. Press the Manual button and adjust the timer to 10 minutes. When the timer beeps, quick-release pressure until float valve drops and then unlock lid. Serve garnished with parsley if desired.

Veggie "Pot Roast"

Appliances like the Instant Pot® sometimes seem to have been invented just to make pot roasts. We've learned to make them do so much more, of course, but this Veggie "Pot Roast" speaks to the soul of any longtime pressure-cooker cook. Throw potatoes, carrots, or other vegetables into the mix to make this an even more complete meal.

- **Hands-On Time: 25 minutes**
- **Cook Time: 30 minutes**

Serves 4

1¾ cups whole-wheat flour

1¾ cups unbleached white flour

1¾ cups cold water, as needed

3½ cups vegetable broth

2 tablespoons olive oil

1 medium yellow onion, peeled and sliced

1 cup sliced button or cremini mushrooms

1 tablespoon soy sauce

1 (12-ounce) beer of your choice

2 tablespoons all-purpose flour

Pinch salt

Pinch freshly ground black pepper

1. Place the whole-wheat and unbleached flour in a large mixing bowl and stir well to combine. While stirring, gradually add the cold water to form a sticky dough. Form the dough into a ball and knead 15 minutes. Cover the dough with cold water, place in the refrigerator, and keep submerged at least 30 minutes.

2. Transfer the dough to a colander and place it in the sink. Under cold running water, carefully knead the dough, rinsing out the starch and bran. After several minutes, the gluten will start to stick together. Alternate between room-temperature water and cold-water rinses while continuing to knead the dough until it has a firm, rubbery texture.

3. Pour the broth into the Instant Pot®. Tear apart pieces of the dough and form into 1" balls (about the size of Ping-Pong balls). Drop the balls of dough into the liquid one at a time, stirring occasionally to prevent sticking. Lock the lid into place. Press the Manual button and adjust timer to 20 minutes.

4. When the timer beeps, quick-release pressure until the valve floats and then unlock lid. Remove the seitan and drain the remaining liquid from the pot. Chop the seitan into bite-sized pieces.

continued on next page

Veggie "Pot Roast"—*continued*

5 Press the Sauté button on the pot and add the oil. Sauté the onions and mushrooms about 5 minutes until tender.

6 Add the seitan, soy sauce, and beer. Press the Manual button on the pot and set the timer for 7 minutes. When the timer beeps, quick-release pressure until valve drops and then unlock lid.

7 Remove the seitan, onions, and mushrooms from the pot and place on a serving plate, but leave the liquid in the pot. Press the Sauté button and adjust temperature to Low. Bring the remaining liquid to a simmer. Gradually stir in the flour to create a gravy. Add salt and pepper.

8 Pour gravy over seitan on plate and serve.

Smoked Portobello and Seitan

If you don't have red wine in the house or don't drink alcohol, it's no problem, but it's best not to simply eliminate it or, as some cooks do, to substitute it with water. Consider vegetable broth or, if you're feeling daring, cranberry juice instead—you'll notice the difference, but the flavors will still excite.

- **Hands-On Time: 25 minutes**
- **Cook Time: 28 minutes**

Serves 4

1¾ cups whole-wheat flour

1¾ cups unbleached white flour

1¾ cups cold water, as needed

3½ cups vegetable broth

1 tablespoon olive oil

1 medium yellow onion, peeled and chopped

3 portobello mushroom caps, chopped

1 tablespoon soy sauce

¼ teaspoon liquid smoke

½ cup dry red wine

2–4 tablespoons all-purpose flour

Pinch salt

Pinch freshly ground black pepper

2 tablespoons chopped fresh Italian flat-leaf parsley

1 Place the whole-wheat and unbleached flour in a large mixing bowl and stir well to combine. While stirring, gradually pour enough water into the flour to form a sticky dough that can be kneaded. Form the dough into a ball and knead 15 minutes. Cover the dough with cold water, place in the refrigerator, and keep submerged at least 30 minutes.

2 Transfer the dough to a colander and place it in the sink. Under cold running water, carefully knead the dough, rinsing out the starch and bran. After several minutes of cold-water rinsing and kneading, the gluten will start to stick together. Alternate between room-temperature water and cold-water rinses while continuing to knead the dough until it has a firm, rubbery texture.

3 Pour the broth into the Instant Pot®. Tear apart pieces of the dough and form into 1" balls (about the size of Ping-Pong balls). Drop the balls of dough into the liquid one at a time, stirring occasionally to prevent sticking.

4 Lock the lid into place, press the Manual button, and adjust timer to 20 minutes. When the timer beeps, quick-release pressure until float valve drops and then unlock lid. Remove the seitan and drain the remaining liquid from the pot. Chop the seitan into bite-sized pieces.

continued on next page

Smoked Portobello and Seitan—*continued*

5 Press the Sauté button on the pot and add the olive oil. Sauté the onions and mushrooms until tender. Add the seitan, soy sauce, liquid smoke, and red wine and allow to simmer 2–3 minutes. Remove the seitan, onions, and mushrooms with a slotted spoon, leaving the juices behind.

6 Gradually add the all-purpose flour, stirring to make a gravy. When the gravy is done, drizzle it over the seitan mixture. Add the salt and pepper and garnish with parsley. Serve.

Indian Seitan Curry

The combination of curry and cayenne give this dish some spice. To tone it down a bit for young or sensitive palates, dial back the cayenne to ⅛ teaspoon or exclude it entirely—most of the flavor here emerges from the curry powder in any event, so most diners won't notice a difference.

- **Hands-On Time: 25 minutes**
- **Cook Time: 33 minutes**

Serves 4

1¾ cups whole-wheat flour
1¾ cups unbleached white flour
1¾ cups cold water, as needed
3½ cups vegetable broth
2 tablespoons olive oil
½ medium yellow onion, peeled and chopped
2 cloves garlic, minced
1 teaspoon minced fresh ginger
3 tablespoons curry powder
1 teaspoon paprika
1 teaspoon granulated sugar
½ teaspoon cayenne pepper
1 teaspoon soy sauce
1 (13.5-ounce) can coconut milk
Pinch salt
Pinch freshly ground black pepper

1 Place the whole-wheat and unbleached flour in a large mixing bowl and stir well to combine. While stirring, gradually pour enough water into the flour to form a sticky dough that can be kneaded. Form the dough into a ball and knead 15 minutes. Cover the dough with cold water and refrigerate 30 minutes.

2 Transfer the dough to a colander and place it in the sink. Under cold running water, carefully knead the dough, rinsing out the starch and bran. After several minutes of cold-water rinsing and kneading, the gluten will start to stick together. Continue to knead the dough until it has a firm, rubbery texture.

3 Pour the broth into the Instant Pot®. Tear apart pieces of the dough and form into 1" balls (about the size of Ping-Pong balls). Drop the balls of dough into the liquid one at a time, stirring occasionally to prevent sticking. Lock the lid into place. Press the Manual button and adjust timer to 20 minutes.

4 When the timer beeps, quick-release pressure until the valve floats and then unlock lid. Remove the seitan, and drain the remaining liquid from the pot. Chop the seitan into bite-sized pieces.

5 Press the Sauté button on the pot and add the olive oil. Sauté the onion until it turns a golden color. Add the garlic and ginger and sauté 1 minute more. Add the seitan and all remaining ingredients and let simmer 10 minutes. Serve warm.

Black Pepper Seitan and Broccoli

Modeled after the popular Chinese dish, this recipe can be served with white or brown rice. Those avoiding wheat gluten can enjoy this meal by substituting gluten-free flours and using tamari, a wheat-free soy sauce found in most grocery stores.

- **Hands-On Time: 25 minutes**
- **Cook Time: 25 minutes**

Serves 4

1¾ cups whole-wheat flour

1¾ cups unbleached white flour

1¾ cups cold water, as needed

3½ cups vegetable broth

2 tablespoons vegetable oil

1 medium yellow onion, peeled and sliced

2 cloves garlic, minced

2 cups chopped broccoli, blanched

2 tablespoons soy sauce

1 teaspoon freshly ground black pepper

½ teaspoon granulated sugar

SPICE IT UP

The herbs and spices in this recipe are kept to a minimum, but you can add more flavor if you'd like. Add 1 teaspoon cayenne pepper for a little kick and ½ teaspoon ginger or Chinese five-spice powder for added flavor.

1 Place the whole-wheat and unbleached flour in a large mixing bowl and stir well to combine. While stirring, gradually pour enough water into the flour to form a sticky dough that can be kneaded. Form the dough into a ball and knead 15 minutes. Cover the dough with cold water and refrigerate 30 minutes.

2 Transfer the dough to a colander and place it in the sink. Under cold running water, carefully knead the dough, rinsing out the starch and bran. After several minutes of cold-water rinsing and kneading, the gluten will start to stick together. Continue to knead the dough until it has a firm, rubbery texture.

3 Pour the broth into the Instant Pot®. Tear apart pieces of the dough and form into 1" balls (about the size of Ping-Pong balls). Drop the balls into the liquid one at a time, stirring occasionally to prevent sticking. Lock the lid into place. Press the Manual button and adjust timer to 20 minutes.

4 When the timer beeps, quick-release pressure until float valve drops and then unlock lid. Remove the seitan and drain the remaining liquid from the pot. Chop the seitan into bite-sized pieces.

5 Press the Sauté button and add the oil to the pot. Sauté the onions until lightly caramelized. Add the garlic, seitan, and broccoli and sauté 1 minute more. Add the soy sauce, black pepper, and sugar. Mix well and sauté an additional 30 seconds before serving.

Burgers

The ease of the Instant Pot® makes cooking beans and grains for vegan burgers a breeze. No longer will you have to rely on frozen patties when you can cook your own ingredients fast and easy and get burgers on the table in no time. The burgers in this chapter will suit whatever mood you are in and whatever flavor you are craving. With recipes using a wide range of ingredients—such as the Brown Rice Burger, Chili Cheeseburger, and Spicy Black Bean Burger—you are sure to find a burger recipe you'll love.

Spicy Black Bean Burger

Thanks to their wide appeal and fantastic nutritional value, black bean burgers are one of the most commonly consumed homemade veggie burgers. Omit the spice from this recipe to use it as a base for your own veggie burger creation.

- **Hands-On Time: 15 minutes**
- **Cook Time: 50 minutes**

Serves 2

2 tablespoons vegetable oil

½ medium yellow onion, peeled and diced

1 medium jalapeño, seeded and minced

3 cloves garlic, minced

2 cups vegetable broth

1 cup dried black beans

1 tablespoon chili powder

1 teaspoon salt

Pinch freshly ground black pepper

1 tablespoon ground cumin

½ cup panko bread crumbs

¼ cup chopped fresh Italian flat-leaf parsley

1 Press the Sauté button on the Instant Pot® and heat the oil. Add the onion and jalapeño, and sauté 3–4 minutes. Add the garlic and sauté 1 minute. Add broth and deglaze the pot by scraping the sides and bottom.

2 Add the beans, chili powder, salt, pepper, and cumin to the pot. Lock the lid into place. Press the Bean button and cook for the default time of 30 minutes. When the timer beeps, let pressure release naturally for 10 minutes. Quick-release any remaining pressure until float valve drops and then unlock lid.

3 Press the Sauté button on the pot and adjust setting to Less. Simmer the bean mixture unlidded 10 minutes to thicken. Transfer the mixture to a large bowl. When cool enough to handle, quickly mix in the panko and parsley.

4 Form into equal-sized patties. Cook on the stovetop over medium heat in a large skillet 2–3 minutes on each side until browned.

5 Remove from heat and enjoy individually or add each patty to a vegan bun of preference. Serve warm.

Pinto Bean Burger

Making homemade burgers can be time-consuming for a busy family, even with many shortcuts and efficient kitchen gadgets. With the Instant Pot®, burger recipes such as this Pinto Bean Burger can be made quickly and easily. Opting for healthy Instant Pot® burger recipes, anyone can create delicious and nutritious varieties of burgers that save time, money, and energy.

- **Hands-On Time: 10 minutes**
- **Cook Time: 40 minutes**

Serves 6

1 cup dried pinto beans
2 cups vegetable broth
3 tablespoons vegetable oil, divided
1 teaspoon salt
1 medium yellow onion, peeled and diced
1 cup chopped walnuts
½ cup rolled oats
2 teaspoons cornstarch combined with 2 tablespoons warm water
¾ cup ketchup
1 teaspoon garlic powder
1 teaspoon dried basil
1 teaspoon dried parsley
Pinch freshly ground black pepper

1 Rinse and then drain the beans.

2 Add the beans, broth, 2 tablespoons oil, salt, and onion to the Instant Pot®. Lock the lid into place. Press the Bean button and let cook for the default time of 30 minutes. When the timer beeps, let pressure release naturally for 10 minutes. Quick-release any remaining pressure until float valve drops and then unlock lid.

3 Press the Sauté button on the pot and adjust setting to Less. Simmer bean mixture unlidded 10 minutes to thicken.

4 Transfer the mixture to a large bowl and mash beans. When cool enough to handle, quickly mix in remaining ingredients and stir to combine well.

5 Form into equal-sized patties and cook on the stovetop in a medium skillet, prepared with 1 tablespoon oil, for 2–3 minutes on each side until browned.

6 Remove from heat and enjoy each patty individually or add each patty to a vegan bun of choice. Serve warm.

Very Vegetable Burger

Roasting—or in the case of your Instant Pot®, sautéing—your Very Vegetable Burger veggies before mixing them into the patty mixture will bring out more flavor in the bell pepper, onion, squash, and zucchini. For a much faster meal, skip the dried beans and pick up a can at the grocer—it'll bring your cooking time down to less than 30 minutes.

- **Hands-On Time: 20 minutes**
- **Cook Time: 55 minutes**

Serves 2

2 tablespoons olive oil, divided
½ medium yellow onion, peeled and chopped
½ medium red bell pepper, seeded and chopped
½ cup chopped yellow squash
½ medium zucchini, chopped
4 cloves garlic, minced
1 cup dried black beans
8 cups water
1 teaspoon salt
½ jalapeño, seeded and minced
½ cup panko bread crumbs
Pinch freshly ground black pepper

1 Press the Sauté button on the Instant Pot® and heat 1 tablespoon oil. Add the onion and pepper; sauté 3 minutes. Add the squash, zucchini, and garlic; sauté 3 minutes. Transfer the onion mixture to a small bowl and set aside.

2 Add the beans, water, and salt to the pot. Lock the lid into place. Press the Bean button and cook for the default time of 30 minutes. When the timer beeps, let pressure release naturally for 10 minutes. Quick-release any remaining pressure until float valve drops and then unlock lid.

3 Press the Sauté button on the pot, adjust setting to Less, and simmer bean mixture unlidded 10 minutes to thicken.

4 Transfer the mixture to a large bowl and mash. When cool enough to handle, quickly mix in the vegetable mixture, jalapeño, panko, and pepper and blend thoroughly.

5 Form into equal-sized patties. Cook on the stovetop in a medium skillet, prepared with 1 tablespoon oil, for 2–3 minutes on each side until browned.

6 Remove from heat and add each patty to a bun. Serve warm.

Brown Rice Burger

Protein and iron are two of the vital nutrients found in this simple Brown Rice Burger. This is one of the simplest and most down-to-earth recipes in this book. For a little extra kick you can always rely on your favorite vegan condiments, or even add a bit more bread crumbs to this mix for a crunchier bite.

- **Hands-On Time: 10 minutes**
- **Cook Time: 40 minutes**

Serves 4

1 cup long-grain brown rice
2 cups water
½ cup chopped button mushrooms
½ cup corn
½ cup peeled and shredded carrot
¼ medium yellow onion, peeled and diced
Pinch salt
Pinch freshly ground black pepper
2 cups bread crumbs
1 tablespoon olive oil

1 Add the rice and water to the Instant Pot®. Press the Rice button and cook for the default time. When the timer beeps, let pressure release naturally until float valve drops and then unlock lid. Fluff the rice with a fork.

2 In a large bowl, combine the cooked rice, mushrooms, corn, carrot, onion, salt, and pepper. Mash the mixture with a potato masher and form into patties. Dredge each patty in bread crumbs and set aside.

3 Add the olive oil to a large frying pan and fry the burgers over medium heat until they are browned, about 2–3 minutes on each side.

Beet Red Burger

Beets will give your burger the appearance of rare meat and a big helping of B vitamins, without all of the fat. At the same time, fat is a binding agent, and vegan burgers can be tough to hold together. If you're finding yours a little loose, try adding a bit more of the cornstarch mixture.

- **Hands-On Time: 10 minutes**
- **Cook Time: 45 minutes**

Serves 4

5 medium beets, quartered

1½ cups water

½ cup chopped yellow onions

1½ cups chopped walnuts

4 teaspoons cornstarch combined with ¼ cup warm water

2 tablespoons soy sauce

1 cup shredded vegan Cheddar cheese

⅛ cup all-purpose flour

2 tablespoons olive oil

Pinch salt

Pinch freshly ground black pepper

1 Add the beets and water to the Instant Pot®. Lock the lid into place, press the Manual button, and adjust timer to 15 minutes. When the timer beeps, let pressure release naturally until float valve drops and then unlock lid.

2 Drain the beets and add to a large bowl. Add the remaining ingredients and mash the mixture with a potato masher. Form the beet mixture into burger patties.

3 Preheat the oven to 350°F. Spray a large baking sheet with cooking spray.

4 Place the patties on the prepared baking sheet and bake 25–30 minutes.

BBQ Tempeh Burger

It's recommended that you always marinate tempeh or cook it in liquid for optimal results. If you don't, it can easily become too dry to eat. Fortunately, either approach is a snap with your Instant Pot®. This BBQ Tempeh Burger will run too hot for some tastes, too mild for others—as always, a great place to make the adjustment is in the cayenne pepper portion, which starts here at a relatively mild ⅛ teaspoon.

- **Hands-On Time: 10 minutes**
- **Cook Time: 60 minutes**

Serves 4

1 cup red lentils
8 ounces tempeh, crumbled
4½ cups water
1 tablespoon vegetable oil
1 teaspoon salt
½ cup all-purpose flour
½ cup Dijon mustard
¼ cup granulated sugar
⅛ cup light brown sugar
¼ cup apple cider vinegar
1 tablespoon chili powder
⅛ teaspoon cayenne pepper
½ teaspoon soy sauce
1 tablespoon vegan margarine
½ tablespoon liquid smoke
Pinch freshly ground black pepper

1 Preheat the oven to 350°F. Grease a large baking sheet with cooking spray.

2 Add the lentils, tempeh, water, oil, and salt to the Instant Pot®. Lock the lid into place and cook for the default time of 30 minutes. When the timer beeps, let pressure release naturally until float valve drops and then unlock lid. Drain the lentils and tempeh, and add to a large mixing bowl.

3 Combine the rest of the ingredients with the lentils and tempeh. Mash the mixture with a potato masher. Form the mixture into burger patties.

4 Place the burgers on the prepared baking sheet. Bake 25–30 minutes, flipping after 15 minutes.

Tropical Veggie Burger

Many believe red lentils to be the best burger substitute in the vegan world and, once you taste this Tropical Veggie Burger, you're sure to agree. To tone down this flavor-rich burger, you can always skip one or more of the spices. Allspice might be a good place to hold back, as even some adventurous eaters find the flavor overpowering.

- **Hands-On Time: 10 minutes**
- **Cook Time: 50 minutes**

Serves 2

1½ tablespoons vegan margarine

1 medium yellow onion, peeled and chopped

4 teaspoons curry powder

⅓ cup peeled and shredded carrots

2 tablespoons dry white wine

1 cup red lentils

¼ cup brown rice

5 cups water

2 tablespoons vegetable oil, divided

1 teaspoon salt

2 tablespoons hot sauce

½ cup panko bread crumbs

4 cloves garlic, minced

4 teaspoons minced fresh ginger

½ teaspoon ground allspice

1 teaspoon ground cumin

1. Press the Sauté button on the Instant Pot® and add the margarine. Sauté the onion about 5 minutes until it begins to brown. Add the curry powder, carrots, and white wine. Sauté 1 minute longer. Transfer the mixture to a small bowl and set aside.

2. Add the lentils, brown rice, water, 1 tablespoon oil, and salt to the pot. Lock the lid, press the Rice button, and cook for the default time. When the timer beeps, let pressure release naturally until float valve drops and then unlock lid.

3. Pour the lentils and rice into a large bowl and add the rest of the ingredients except the remaining oil. Mash the mixture with a potato masher. Form the bean mixture into burger patties.

4. Add the remaining oil to a medium skillet over medium-high heat and cook the burgers until they are browned on both sides, about 2–3 minutes on each side.

SERVING SUGGESTIONS
Typical burger toppings, such as ketchup and mustard, might not be the best condiments for this burger. Try topping it with a grilled pineapple ring or mango salsa.

Bulgur-Nut Burger

For those serious about eating whole, natural vegan foods while keeping calories down, this Bulgur-Nut Burger is a candidate to crack the regular meal rotation. It is simple on its own, so most will want to top it with avocado slices or other traditional toppings like lettuce, tomato, and vegan cheese.

- **Hands-On Time: 10 minutes**
- **Cook Time: 30 minutes**

Serves 4

2 tablespoons olive oil, divided
½ cup diced yellow onion
2 cloves garlic, minced
2 cups canned pinto beans, rinsed and drained
1 cup bulgur
3 cups vegetable broth
¾ cup walnuts
½ cup chopped fresh cilantro
1 teaspoon ground cumin
¼ teaspoon cayenne pepper

1 Press the Sauté pan on the Instant Pot® and add 1 tablespoon olive oil. Add the onion and sauté about 3 minutes until it begins to brown. Add the garlic and sauté 1 minute more. Add the pinto beans and cook until the beans are tender, about 5 minutes. Add a little water if needed.

2 Add the bulgur and broth to the pot. Lock the lid into place, press the Manual button, and adjust timer to 15 minutes. When the timer beeps, let pressure release naturally until float valve drops and then unlock lid.

3 In a large bowl, combine all the ingredients except the remaining oil. Put the mixture in a food processor and pulse until finely chopped. Form the mixture into patties.

4 Add remaining olive oil to a frying pan over medium-high heat and fry the patties until browned, about 2–3 minutes on each side.

Onion, Mushroom, and "Cheese"-Stuffed Burger

To make the Onion, Mushroom, and "Cheese"-Stuffed Burger in a hurry, use canned beans instead of dried ones. Just cook for 1 minute to warm through. Remember to adjust that cooking time accordingly. If you go with dried beans and cook them the full half hour the results will be quite different, though!

- **Hands-On Time: 10 minutes**
- **Cook Time: 35 minutes**

Serves 2

1 cup dried black beans

½ medium yellow onion, peeled and diced

3 tablespoons vegetable oil, divided

1 teaspoon salt

4 cups water

2 cups chopped button mushrooms

2 cloves garlic, minced

¾ cup panko bread crumbs

½ tablespoon ground cumin

1 teaspoon chili powder

½ teaspoon dried thyme

Pinch freshly ground black pepper

4 slices vegan mozzarella

1 Add the beans, onions, 1 tablespoon oil, salt, and water to the Instant Pot®. Lock the lid into place, press the Bean button, and let cook for the default time of 30 minutes. When the timer beeps, let pressure release naturally until float valve drops and then unlock lid.

2 Pour the beans into a large bowl and add the rest of the ingredients, except the remaining oil and the cheese. Mash the mixture with a potato masher. Fold a slice of cheese in half and form the patties around the cheese to make a stuffed burger.

3 Add the rest of the oil to a large skillet over medium-high heat and cook the burgers until browned on both sides, about 2–3 minutes per side.

Smoked Portobello Burger

Portobello mushroom caps can be cooked in the Instant Pot®, a traditional pressure cooker, on a stove top, on a grill, or in the oven. One great benefit of the Instant Pot® for this Smoked Portobello Burger is that if you're pressed for time, the quick cooking allows you to cut back or eliminate the marinating time completely.

- **Hands-On Time: 5 minutes**
- **Cook Time: 10 minutes**

Serves 4

4 large portobello mushroom caps

¼ cup red wine vinegar

2 tablespoons extra-virgin olive oil

1 tablespoon minced shallots

½ tablespoon soy sauce

Pinch salt

Pinch freshly ground black pepper

1 cup water

1 tablespoon liquid smoke

1 Place the mushroom caps in a shallow dish. In a small bowl, mix together the vinegar, oil, shallots, soy sauce, salt, and pepper. Pour the mixture over the mushrooms and let marinate about 20 minutes, turning 2–3 times throughout.

2 Pour the water and liquid smoke into the Instant Pot®, place the steamer tray inside, and place the mushrooms on top of the steamer tray. Lock the lid into place, press the Steam button on the pot, and cook for the default time of 10 minutes. When the timer beeps, quick-release pressure until float valve drops and then unlock lid.

3 Remove portobellos and serve warm.

LIQUID SMOKE

Liquid smoke helps give food a true barbecue flavor without the hassle of traditional barbecue cooking. It's often sold in small bottles on the condiment aisle (near steak sauce, ketchup, and mustard), or can be ordered online. Use liquid smoke by combining with a liquid when cooking, or brush directly onto ingredients such as mushrooms or veggie burgers.

South of the Border Burger

Consider the flavors of Mexico when deciding on toppings for this festive South of the Border Burger and try avocado, pickled jalapeño slices, or even salsa. It may take some time to get the hang of preparing burgers start-to-finish with your Instant Pot®, but once you do, you'll likely never go back.

- **Hands-On Time: 10 minutes**
- **Cook Time: 40 minutes**

Serves 2

3 tablespoons vegetable oil, divided

½ medium green bell pepper, seeded and chopped

½ medium yellow onion, peeled and diced

3 cloves garlic, minced

1 cup dried black beans

4 cups water

1 teaspoon salt

2 teaspoons cornstarch combined with 2 tablespoons warm water

1 tablespoon ground cumin

1 teaspoon chipotle chili powder

½ cup salsa

½ cup panko bread crumbs

Pinch salt

Pinch freshly ground black pepper

1 Press the Sauté button on the Instant Pot® and add 1 tablespoon oil. Sauté the bell pepper and onion 3–4 minutes. Add the garlic and sauté 1 more minute. Transfer onion mixture to a small bowl and set aside.

2 Add the beans, 1 tablespoon oil, water, and salt to the pot. Lock the lid into place, press the Bean button, and cook for the default time of 30 minutes. When the timer beeps, quick-release pressure until float valve drops and then unlock lid.

3 Combine all of the ingredients except remaining oil and mash with a potato masher and form the mixture into patties.

4 Add the remaining oil to a large skillet and cook the burgers until they are brown on both sides, about 2–3 minutes per side.

Chili Cheeseburger

If you're short on time, try using a store-bought vegetarian chili, such as Hormel's vegetarian canned chili. There are a lot of ingredients and steps in this or any Chili Cheeseburger—take the plunge, and the summer appetites in your life will thank you for it.

- **Hands-On Time: 10 minutes**
- **Cook Time: 35 minutes**

Serves 6

2 tablespoons vegetable oil, divided

½ medium white onion, peeled and diced

1 jalapeño, seeded and minced

3 cloves garlic, minced

1 cup dried black beans

4 cups water

1 teaspoon salt

1 tablespoon chili powder

1 tablespoon ground cumin

½ cup panko bread crumbs

¼ cup chopped fresh Italian flat-leaf parsley

Pinch salt

Pinch freshly ground black pepper

6 vegan hamburger buns

6 slices vegan Cheddar cheese

2 cups Speedy Chili con "Carne" (see recipe in Chapter 5)

1 Press the Sauté button on the Instant Pot® and add 1 tablespoon oil. Add the onion and jalapeño, and sauté 3–4 minutes. Add the garlic and sauté 1 more minute. Transfer the onion mixture to a small bowl and set aside.

2 Add the beans, water, and salt to the Instant Pot®. Lock the lid into place, press the Bean button, and let cook for the default time of 30 minutes. When the timer beeps, let pressure release naturally until float valve drops and then unlock lid.

3 Add the remaining ingredients except remaining oil, buns, cheese, and chili. Mash the bean mixture with a potato masher and form the bean mixture into burger patties.

4 Add the remaining oil to a large skillet over medium-high heat and cook the burgers until browned on both sides, about 2–3 minutes per side.

5 Place 1 patty on each hamburger bun and top with a slice of cheese. Melt the cheese under a broiler or in the microwave for a few seconds, then top with a scoop of chili.

"Bacon" and Avocado Burger

You should be able to find plenty of tasty vegetarian "bacon" options for your "Bacon" and Avocado Burger at your local health food store or even at a more traditional grocery store chain near you. Use one of those fast-cooking options if you don't have time to make your own.

- **Hands-On Time: 10 minutes**
- **Cook Time: 40 minutes**

Serves 4

3 tablespoons vegetable oil, divided

½ medium yellow onion, peeled and diced

1 medium jalapeño, seeded and minced

3 cloves garlic, minced

1 cup dried black beans

1 tablespoon chili powder

1 tablespoon ground cumin

4 cups water

1 teaspoon salt

½ cup panko bread crumbs

¼ cup fresh Italian flat-leaf parsley

Pinch freshly ground black pepper

8–12 pieces cooked vegan bacon, such as Tempeh Bacon

1 medium avocado, peeled, pitted, and sliced

1 Select the Sauté button on the Instant Pot® and add 1 tablespoon oil, onion, and jalapeño, and sauté 3–4 minutes. Add garlic and sauté 1 more minute. Transfer the onion mixture to a small glass bowl and set aside.

2 Add the beans, chili powder, cumin, 1 tablespoon oil, and water to the pot. Lock the lid into place and press the Bean button. Cook for the default time of 30 minutes. When the timer beeps, quick-release pressure until float valve drops and then unlock lid.

3 Combine the beans and onion mixture in a bowl and add the rest of the ingredients except vegan bacon and avocado. Mash the mixture with a potato masher. Form the bean mixture into burger patties.

4 Add the remaining 1 tablespoon oil to a large skillet over medium-high heat and cook the burgers until browned on both sides, about 2–3 minutes per side.

5 Top each burger with vegan bacon and avocado slices.

Quinoa Burger

Quinoa is a grain popular with some vegans and vegetarians thanks to its high protein and iron content and fast cooking time. Still somewhat underappreciated—who among us hasn't heard or even made a quinoa joke in recent years—quinoa is of course not a new food at all, but in fact one of the most ancient grains still under human cultivation.

- **Hands-On Time: 10 minutes**
- **Cook Time: 50 minutes**

Serves 2

½ cup quinoa

1 cup water

1 medium carrot, peeled and shredded

½ medium yellow onion, peeled and diced

2 (15-ounce) cans white beans, drained

2 teaspoons cornstarch combined with 2 tablespoons warm water

1 tablespoon ground cumin

1 teaspoon dried sage or basil

Pinch salt

Pinch freshly ground black pepper

1 tablespoon olive oil

1 Add the quinoa and water to the Instant Pot®. Lock the lid into place, press the Multigrain button, and let cook for the default time of 40 minutes. When the timer beeps, quick-release pressure until float valve drops and then unlock lid.

2 Fluff the quinoa with a fork. In a large bowl, combine the quinoa with all remaining ingredients except olive oil. Mash the mixture with a potato masher. Form the mixture into patties.

3 Add the olive oil to a large skillet over medium-high heat and cook the burgers until browned, about 2–3 minutes per side.

10

Desserts

If you're like most people, you probably have a sweet tooth that pulls at your stomach from time to time. The great thing about the Instant Pot® is that it creates desserts that are just the right size to make both your sweet tooth and your scale happy. Most of these desserts provide only 4–6 servings, so you won't be tempted to over-eat and you won't have desserts hanging around your kitchen for days on end. And with dishes ranging from Glazed Lemon Poppy Seed Cake and Banana Pudding Cake to Spiced Peaches and Fruit Compote, these perfect little delights are guaranteed to hit the spot...no matter what you find yourself craving.

Savory Sun-Dried Tomato Cheesecake

If you've never tried a rich, savory cheesecake—or even if you have—you're in for a treat. You can freeze this cheesecake up to 3 months, so it makes the perfect make-ahead addition for a cheese plate. Thaw a wedge of Savory Sun-Dried Tomato Cheesecake in the refrigerator and then serve at room temperature to spread on crackers or thin slices of crusty bread.

- **Hands-On Time: 5 minutes**
- **Cook Time: 30 minutes**

Yields 7" cheesecake

3 tablespoons vegan margarine, melted

⅓ cup bread crumbs or savory cracker crumbs

½ cup sun-dried tomatoes in oil

6 cloves garlic, minced

1 teaspoon dried oregano

3 ounces silken soft tofu

3 tablespoons all-purpose flour

18 ounces vegan cream cheese

¾ cup vegan sour cream, divided

½ cup diced green onion

2 cups hot water

1 Grease a 7" springform pan.

2 **For crust:** Combine the melted margarine and crumbs, then evenly distribute the crumbs over the bottom and sides of the prepared pan. Place a 16" × 16" piece of plastic wrap on top of an equal-sized piece of aluminum foil. Put the pan in the center of the plastic wrap–topped foil; form and crimp the foil around the pan to seal the bottom.

3 **For the cheesecake filling:** Drain the tomatoes, leaving 1 tablespoon oil, and add to a food processor along with the garlic, oregano, silken tofu, flour, cream cheese, and ¼ cup sour cream. Purée until smooth. Stir in the green onions. Pour into the springform pan. Cover with foil; crimp to seal.

4 Pour the water into the Instant Pot®. Insert the trivet. Set the springform pan on the trivet. Lock the lid into place. Press the Manual button and adjust timer to 30 minutes. When the timer beeps, quick-release pressure until float valve drops and then unlock lid. Lift the pan out of the pot. Let cool.

5 Spread the remaining ½ cup sour cream over the top. Refrigerate a minimum of 2 hours before serving.

Cranberry Applesauce

Cranberries have become much more affordable in recent years, making this applesauce as thrifty as it is quick. As with any dish, make sure that the ingredients don't go above the halfway mark on the Instant Pot®.

- **Hands-On Time: 5 minutes**
- **Cook Time: 7 minutes**

Serves 8

1 cup cranberries

4 medium tart apples, peeled, cored, and grated

4 medium sweet apples, peeled, cored, and grated

Zest and juice from 1 large orange

½ cup dark brown sugar

½ cup granulated sugar

1 tablespoon vegan margarine

2 teaspoons ground cinnamon

½ teaspoon ground cloves

¼ teaspoon freshly ground black pepper

⅛ teaspoon salt

1 tablespoon fresh lemon juice

1 Add the cranberries to the Instant Pot® and top with grated apples. Add the remaining ingredients to the pot to cover the cranberries and apples. Lock the lid into place, press the Manual button, and adjust timer to 7 minutes. When the timer beeps, let pressure release naturally until float valve drops and then unlock lid.

2 Lightly mash the apples with a fork. Stir well. Serve warm or chilled.

Coconut Rice

The combination of coconut, currants, and spices transforms this rice into a succulent dish. It pairs especially well with a curry entrée, and is often served that way in East and Southeast Asia, where it originated. It took Instant Pot®, however, to turn this into a 20-minute dish.

- **Hands-On Time: 10 minutes**
- **Cook Time: 20 minutes**

Serves 4

2 tablespoons vegetable oil

1 cup extra-long-grain white rice, rinsed and drained

½ cup unsweetened coconut flakes

2¼ cups water

¼ cup currants

½ teaspoon ground cinnamon

1 teaspoon anise seeds

⅛ teaspoon ground cloves

½ teaspoon salt

1 Press the Sauté button on the Instant Pot® and add the oil. Add the rice, stirring well to coat in the fat.

2 Add the coconut, water, currants, cinnamon, anise seeds, cloves, and salt. Lock the lid into place, press the Manual button, and adjust timer to 20 minutes.

3 When the timer beeps, let pressure drop naturally for 7 minutes. Quick-release any remaining pressure until float valve drops and then unlock lid. Fluff the rice with a fork. Drain off any excess moisture. Serve.

Spiced Peaches

To make spiced peach butter, after Step 2, process the peaches and liquid in a blender or food processor until smooth and return to the Instant Pot®. Simmer and stir over low heat for 30 minutes or until thickened enough to coat the back of a spoon.

- **Hands-On Time: 5 minutes**
- **Cook Time: 10 minutes**

Serves 6

2 (15-ounce) cans sliced peaches in syrup

¼ cup water

1 tablespoon white wine vinegar

⅛ teaspoon ground allspice

1 cinnamon stick

4 whole cloves

½ teaspoon ground ginger

Pinch cayenne pepper

1 tablespoon minced candied ginger (optional)

3 whole black peppercorns (optional)

1 Add all the ingredients to the Instant Pot® and stir to combine thoroughly. Lock the lid into place, press the Manual button, and adjust timer to 5 minutes. When the timer beeps, quick-release the pressure until float valve drops and then unlock lid.

2 Remove and discard the cinnamon stick, cloves, and peppercorns if used.

3 Press the Sauté button on the pot and adjust setting to Low. Simmer and stir 5 minutes to thicken the syrup.

4 Serve warm or chilled. To store, let cool and then refrigerate up to 1 week.

Special Occasion Chunky Applesauce

To sweeten this applesauce, stir in sugar or maple syrup to taste after you remove the lid. At 6 minutes of cooking time, you'll be tempted to whip up this Special Occasion Chunky Applesauce for just about any occasion, or no occasion at all.

- **Hands-On Time: 5 minutes**
- **Cook Time: 6 minutes**

Serves 6

8 Granny Smith apples, peeled, cored, and diced

1 cup apple juice or cider

2 tablespoons fresh lemon juice

¼ cup granulated sugar

⅓ cup packed light brown sugar

½ teaspoon ground nutmeg

¼ teaspoon ground cinnamon

⅓ cup cinnamon hearts candy

1 In the Instant Pot®, combine the apples, apple juice or cider, lemon juice, sugar, brown sugar, nutmeg, and cinnamon, and stir well. Lock the lid into place, press the Manual button, and adjust timer to 6 minutes. When the timer beeps, let pressure release naturally for 10 minutes. Quick-release any remaining pressure until float valve drops and then unlock lid.

2 Stir in the candy until it's melted and blended into the sauce, mashing the apples slightly as you do so.

3 Serve warm or chilled. Can be stored several days in the refrigerator.

Cranberry Sauce

Cranberry Sauce—it's not just for Thanksgiving anymore. The delicious and underappreciated berries are packed with antioxidants and vitamin C, and Instant Pot® can turn this dish around quicker than you could run out to the store for the canned stuff. To bring in even more flavor, stir in some orange liqueur, bourbon, or brandy.

- **Hands-On Time: 5 minutes**
- **Cook Time: 10 minutes**

Serves 6

1 (12-ounce) bag fresh cranberries, rinsed and drained

1 cup granulated sugar

½ cup water, apple juice, or pineapple juice

Pinch salt

1 tablespoon frozen orange juice concentrate

Cinnamon and ground cloves, to taste (optional)

1 In the Instant Pot®, combine the cranberries, sugar, water or juice, and salt. Stir to combine. Lock the lid into place, press the Manual button, and adjust timer to 8 minutes.

2 When the timer beeps, let pressure release naturally for 10 minutes. Quick-release any remaining pressure until float valve drops and then unlock lid.

3 Add the orange juice concentrate. Stir well, breaking the cranberries apart with a spoon or mashing them slightly with a potato masher.

4 Taste for seasoning and adjust if necessary, stirring in additional sugar if needed and the cinnamon and cloves if desired. Serve warm or chilled.

Apple Butter

Less common on American dinner tables than it once was, Apple Butter is essentially an applesauce reduction, its flavors more concentrated and yes, sweeter, than its more ubiquitous cousin. Note that most of the cooking time here is in the sauté—be sure to stir frequently while it's cooking to prevent burning.

- **Hands-On Time: 45 minutes**
- **Cook Time: 45 minutes**

Yields about 2 cups

1 cup apple juice or cider
12 medium Granny Smith
  apples (about 3 pounds),
  peeled, cored, and diced
1½ teaspoons ground
  cinnamon
½ teaspoon ground allspice
⅛ teaspoon ground cloves
1½ cups granulated sugar
1–2 drops cinnamon oil
  (optional)

1 In the Instant Pot®, combine the apple juice or cider and apples. Lock the lid into place, press the Manual button, and adjust timer to 5 minutes. When the timer beeps, let pressure release naturally for 10 minutes. Quick-release any remaining pressure until float valve drops and then unlock lid.

2 Press cooled apples through a fine sieve or food mill, or process in a food processor or blender. Return apples and liquids to the pot, and add the cinnamon, allspice, cloves, sugar, and cinnamon oil, if using.

3 Press the Sauté button and adjust to Low. Simmer the mixture uncovered and stir until the sugar is dissolved. Reduce heat, simmer on low, and allow to thicken 30 minutes. Note that it's important that you frequently stir the apple butter from the bottom of the pan to prevent it from burning.

Dried Fruit Compote

If you plan to add sugar to the Dried Fruit Compote, do so as soon as your Instant Pot® is safe to open and before the fruit has cooled, so that it can be stirred into the fruit mixture until it dissolves.

- **Hands-On Time: 5 minutes**
- **Cook Time: 15 minutes**

Serves 6

1 (8-ounce) package dried apricots

1 (8-ounce) package dried peaches

1 cup golden raisins

1½ cups orange juice

1 cinnamon stick

4 whole cloves

2 tablespoons light brown sugar, to taste (optional)

1   Cut the dried apricots and peaches into quarters and add them to the Instant Pot® along with the raisins, orange juice, cinnamon stick, and cloves. Lock the lid into place and press the Manual button; adjust timer to 5 minutes. When the timer beeps, let pressure release naturally until float valve drops and then unlock lid.

2   Remove the cinnamon stick and cloves. Press the Sauté button on the pot and adjust to Low. Simmer the compote several minutes until desired consistency is achieved.

3   Add sugar to taste, if using, then serve warm or allow to cool. Cover and store in the refrigerator up to 1 week.

Spiced Chocolate Cake

The Instant Pot® consistently amazes with its reduced cooking times, and rarely more so than with this 30-minute Spiced Chocolate Cake. Serve with icing, powdered sugar, or ice cream on top—and of course, adjust the cayenne pepper to taste, as a teaspoon goes a long way.

- **Hands-On Time: 5 minutes**
- **Cook Time: 30 minutes**

Serves 10

1½ cups all-purpose flour
¼ cup cocoa powder
1 teaspoon ground cinnamon
1 teaspoon cayenne pepper
1 teaspoon granulated sugar
¼ teaspoon salt
1 teaspoon baking powder
2 mashed medium bananas
¼ cup melted vegan
    margarine
1 cup unsweetened soy milk
    or almond milk
2 cups hot water

1 In a medium bowl, mix together the flour, cocoa powder, cinnamon, cayenne, sugar, salt, and baking powder.

2 Place the mashed bananas in a large bowl and add the dry ingredients to the bananas. Slowly stir in the melted margarine and the soy milk. Pour the cake mixture into a greased 8" round pan.

3 Pour the hot water into the Instant Pot® and place the trivet inside the pot. Place the cake on the trivet and lock the lid into place. Press the Manual button and adjust timer to 20 minutes.

4 When the timer beeps, let pressure release naturally for 5 minutes. Quick-release any remaining pressure until float valve drops and then unlock lid.

5 Carefully remove the cake from the pot and let cool.

Fruit Compote

Compote can be traced all the way back to medieval Europe, where it was thought to counter the negative effects of humidity. Serve Fruit Compote as a topping for plain or soy yogurt, especially at dessert.

- **Hands-On Time: 8 minutes**
- **Cook Time: 15 minutes**

Serves 6

1 cup apple juice

1 cup dry white wine

2 tablespoons granulated sugar

1 cinnamon stick

¼ teaspoon ground nutmeg

Zest of 1 medium lemon

Zest of 1 medium orange

3 medium Granny Smith apples, peeled, cored, and chopped

3 medium Bartlett pears, peeled, cored, and chopped

½ cup dried cherries, cranberries, or raisins

1. In the Instant Pot®, combine the apple juice and wine, press the Sauté button, and adjust setting to High. Bring to a boil and stir in the sugar until dissolved, about 3 minutes. Add the cinnamon stick, nutmeg, lemon zest, and orange zest. Adjust to Low and simmer 5 minutes.

2. Add the apples and pears to the pot and stir to mix ingredients. Lock the lid into place, press the Manual button, and adjust timer to 3 minutes. When the timer beeps, quick-release pressure until float valve drops and then unlock lid.

3. Use a slotted spoon to transfer the cooked fruit to a serving bowl. Press the Sauté button on the pot and adjust to High to bring juices to a boil; boil and stir until reduced to a syrup that will coat the back of a spoon.

4. Stir the dried cherries, cranberries, or raisins in with the cooked fruit in the bowl and pour the syrup over the fruit mixture. Stir to mix. Allow to cool slightly, then cover with plastic wrap and chill overnight in the refrigerator.

Vanilla-Spice Pear Butter

Bartlett pears are light green in color. They are an especially prevalent fruit crop in the Pacific Northwest and begin arriving fresh to market in late summer. Barletts are the right pear for this dish, as they hold up better than most varietals when cooked. For an extra treat, serve Vanilla-Spice Pear Butter on scones or toasted English muffins.

- **Hands-On Time: 15 minutes**
- **Cook Time: 40 minutes**

Yields about 2 cups

6 medium Bartlett pears, peeled, cored, and diced into 1" pieces
¼ cup dry white wine
1 tablespoon fresh lemon juice
¾ cup granulated sugar
2 orange slices
1 lemon slice
2 whole cloves
1 vanilla bean, split lengthwise
1 cinnamon stick
¼ teaspoon ground cardamom
Pinch salt

1. Add the pears, wine, and lemon juice to the Instant Pot®. Lock the lid into place and press the Manual button. Adjust the timer to 8 minutes.

2. When the timer beeps, allow pressure to release naturally for 10 minutes. Quick-release any remaining pressure until the float valve drops and remove the lid. Using an immersion blender, purée the ingredients until smooth.

3. Press the Sauté button on the pot and adjust setting to Low. Add the sugar. Stir and cook until sugar dissolves. Stir in the remaining ingredients and continue cooking and stirring about 30 minutes or until mixture thickens and mounds slightly on a spoon.

4. Remove and discard the orange and lemon slices, cloves, and cinnamon stick. Remove the vanilla pod; use the back of a knife to scrape away any vanilla seeds still clinging to the pod and stir them into the pear butter. Cover and refrigerate up to 10 days or freeze up to 4 months.

Banana Pudding Cake

This is a delicious way to make the best of overripe bananas. Unlike some pressure cookers, your Instant Pot® is large enough to hold the 1-quart or 6-cup Bundt or angel food cake pan needed to make this recipe.

- **Hands-On Time: 10 minutes**
- **Cook Time: 35 minutes**

Serves 12

1 (18.25-ounce) package vegan cake mix

1 (3.5-ounce) package instant vegan pudding mix

4 ounces silken tofu

4 cups water, divided

¼ cup vegetable oil

3 small ripe bananas, mashed

2 cups powdered sugar, sifted

2 tablespoons unsweetened soy milk or almond milk

1 teaspoon vanilla extract

½ cup toasted and chopped walnuts

1 Treat a 1-quart or 6-cup Bundt or angel food cake pan with nonstick spray. Set aside.

2 Add the cake mix and pudding mix to a large mixing bowl; stir to mix. Make a well in the center and add the tofu and pour in 1 cup water, oil, and mashed bananas.

3 Beat on low speed until blended. Scrape bowl and beat another 4 minutes on medium speed. Pour the batter into the prepared pan. Cover tightly with a piece of heavy-duty aluminum foil.

4 Pour 3 cups water into the Instant Pot® and insert the trivet. Lower the cake pan onto the rack. Lock the lid into place, press the Manual button, and adjust timer to 35 minutes.

5 When the timer beeps, quick-release pressure until float valve drops and then unlock lid.

6 Lift the cake pan out of the pot and place on a wire rack to cool 10 minutes, then turn the cake out onto the wire rack to finish cooling.

7 To make the glaze, mix together the powdered sugar, soy milk, and vanilla in a bowl. Drizzle over the top of the cooled cake. Sprinkle the walnuts over the glaze before the glaze dries.

Chocolate-Berry Bread Pudding

Can a sweet dish be healthy and indulgent at once? This pudding gives it a go with berries, hazelnuts, and bananas in the mix alongside the sugar and salt. Remember that bread pudding really requires less-than-fresh bread, so leave those slices out to dry!

- **Hands-On Time: 10 minutes**
- **Cook Time: 20 minutes**

Serves 6

6 slices day-old vegan white bread
½ cup raspberry preserves
½ cup diced dried strawberries or prunes
½ cup chopped hazelnuts
½ cup cocoa powder
½ cup granulated sugar
Pinch salt
2 tablespoons vegan margarine
2 medium bananas, mashed
2 cups unsweetened soy milk or almond milk
2 cups vegan sour cream
1 tablespoon vanilla extract
1 cup water

1 If the crusts on the bread are dark, remove them. If using fresh bread, lightly toast it. Spread raspberry preserves over the bread. Treat a 5-cup heatproof soufflé dish with nonstick spray.

2 Tear the bread into chunks. Layer half the bread in the bottom of the soufflé dish. Sprinkle with dried fruit and chopped hazelnuts. Add remaining bread with preserves.

3 In a medium bowl, whisk together the cocoa, sugar, and salt. Add the margarine and mashed bananas; whisk to mix. Whisk in soy milk, sour cream, and vanilla. Pour half the cocoa mixture over the bread. Tap down the dish and wait several minutes for the bread to absorb the liquid. Pour in the remaining cocoa mixture.

4 Pour the water into the Instant Pot® and insert the trivet. Set the cake on the trivet. Lock the lid into place, press the Manual button, and adjust timer to 20 minutes. When the timer beeps, let pressure release naturally until float valve drops and then unlock lid.

5 Remove the chocolate-berry bread pudding from the pot and place on a rack until ready to serve or until it's cool enough to cover and refrigerate.

Cornmeal Cake

This dish is reminiscent of corn bread, with a sweeter finish. Serve Cornmeal Cake warm with maple syrup or make a maple-infused butter by whisking pats of vegan margarine into heated maple syrup.

- **Hands-On Time: 10 minutes**
- **Cook Time: 22 minutes**

Serves 6

2 cups unsweetened soy milk or almond milk

¼ cup packed light brown sugar

1 teaspoon orange zest

½ cup fine yellow cornmeal

2 ounces silken tofu

2 tablespoons vegan margarine

2 tablespoons orange marmalade

1 cup water

1 Press the Sauté button on the Instant Pot®. Add the soy milk to the pot and bring to a simmer. Stir in the brown sugar; simmer and stir until the milk is at a low boil. Whisk in the orange zest and cornmeal. Simmer and stir 2 minutes. Remove from heat.

2 In a medium bowl, whisk together the tofu, margarine, and orange marmalade. Stir into the cornmeal mixture. Treat a 1-quart soufflé or heatproof glass dish with nonstick spray. Add batter.

3 Pour the water into the Instant Pot® and insert the trivet. Place soufflé dish on the trivet. Lock the lid into place, press the Manual button, and adjust timer to 12 minutes.

4 When the timer beeps, let pressure release naturally for 10 minutes. Quick-release any remaining pressure until float valve drops and then unlock lid. Transfer to a wire rack to cool.

Creamy Coconut Rice Pudding

Rice pudding—often called rice porridge—is a popular and traditional dessert on almost every continent, but this Creamy Coconut Rice Pudding will call to mind the flavors of Southeast Asia. Garnish it with a sprinkling of ground cinnamon and serve with a dollop of soy whip.

- **Hands-On Time: 10 minutes**
- **Cook Time: 25 minutes**

Serves 6

1½ cups Arborio rice, rinsed and drained

2 cups unsweetened soy milk or almond milk

1 (13.5-ounce) can coconut milk

1 cup water

½ cup granulated sugar

2 teaspoons ground cinnamon

½ teaspoon salt

1½ teaspoons vanilla extract

1 cup dried cherries, dried strawberries, or golden raisins

1 Press the Sauté button on the Instant Pot® and adjust setting to High. Add the rice, soy milk, coconut milk, water, sugar, cinnamon, and salt. Cook and stir to dissolve the sugar, and bring all ingredients to a boil. Lock the lid into place, press the Manual button, and adjust timer to 15 minutes.

2 When the timer beeps, quick-release pressure until float valve drops and then unlock lid. Stir in the vanilla and dried fruit. Replace the cover, but do not lock into place. Let stand 15 minutes. Stir and serve.

Lemon Cheesecake

Serve this rich, popular dessert topped with cherry pie filling or sugared fresh blueberries, raspberries, or strawberries. Lemon Cheesecake makes a fantastically decadent summertime dessert, after dinner, or even after lunch.

- **Hands-On Time: 10 minutes**
- **Cook Time: 15 minutes**

Serves 8

12 gingersnaps or vanilla wafers

1½ tablespoons almonds, toasted

½ tablespoon vegan margarine

2 (8-ounce) packages vegan cream cheese

½ cup granulated sugar

2 ounces silken tofu

Zest of 1 medium lemon

1 tablespoon fresh lemon juice

½ teaspoon natural lemon extract

1 teaspoon vanilla extract

2 cups water

1 Grease the inside of a 7" springform pan with nonstick spray.

2 Add the cookies and almonds to a food processor. Pulse to create cookie crumbs and chop the nuts. Add the melted margarine and pulse to mix.

3 Transfer the crumb mixture to the springform pan and press down into the pan.

4 Cut the cream cheese into cubes and add it to the food processor along with the sugar; process until smooth. Add the tofu, lemon zest, lemon juice, lemon extract, and vanilla. Process 10 seconds or until smooth. Scrape the bowl and then process another 10 seconds or until the batter is well mixed and smooth.

5 Place the springform pan in the center of two 16" × 16" pieces of aluminum foil. Crimp the foil to seal the bottom of the pan.

6 Transfer the batter into the springform pan. Pour the water into the Instant Pot® and insert the trivet. Set the pan on the trivet. Lock the lid into place, press the Manual button, and adjust timer to 15 minutes. When the timer beeps, let pressure release naturally until float valve drops and then unlock lid.

7 Lift the covered pan out of the pot and place on a wire rack. Remove the top foil. If any moisture has accumulated on top of the cheesecake, dab it with a piece of paper towel. Let cool and then remove from the springform pan.

Peanut Butter and Fudge Cheesecake

Who doesn't love peanut butter and chocolate? Peanut Butter and Fudge Cheesecake is prepped in a snap and ready in just 20 minutes.

- **Hands-On Time: 5 minutes**
- **Cook Time: 20 minutes**

Serves 8

1 cup unsalted peanuts, toasted

½ cup vanilla wafers

1 tablespoon vegan cocoa powder

3 tablespoons vegan margarine

1 cup peanut butter

2 (8-ounce) packages vegan cream cheese

½ cup packed light brown sugar

½ cup powdered sugar, sifted

2 tablespoons cornstarch

2 ounces silken tofu

¼ cup soy sour cream

1 (12-ounce) package vegan semisweet chocolate chips

2 cups water

1 Add the peanuts, vanilla wafers, and cocoa to a food processor. Pulse to turn mixture into crumbs. Add the margarine. Pulse to mix.

2 Press into the bottom of a 7" springform pan. Set aside. Wipe out the food processor.

3 Add the peanut butter, cream cheese, and brown sugar to the food processor. Process until smooth.

4 Add the powdered sugar and cornstarch to a small bowl; stir to mix well. Add to the food processor with the tofu and sour cream. Process until smooth.

5 Remove the lid and stir in the chocolate chips. Transfer the batter to the springform pan.

6 Wrap the base of the springform pan with heavy-duty aluminum foil. Tear off a 25"-long piece of heavy-duty aluminum foil and treat one side of one 8" end of the foil with non-stick spray. Place the side treated with non-stick spray over the top of the springform pan and then wrap the remaining foil under and then over the pan again; crimp to seal.

7 Pour the water and place the trivet into the Instant Pot®. Place the pan on the rack over the foil strips. Lock the lid and press the Manual button. Adjust the timer to 20 minutes.

8 When the timer beeps, let pressure release naturally until float valve drops and then unlock lid. Place the pan on a wire rack. Allow to cool, and refrigerate 4 hours before serving.

Molten Fudge Pudding Cake

This cake is just about as extravagant as home desserts come. Serve this Molten Fudge Pudding Cake warm with a scoop of soy ice cream and garnish with fresh fruit or dust with powdered sugar.

- **Hands-On Time: 10 minutes**
- **Cook Time: 25 minutes**

Serves 6

4 ounces vegan semisweet chocolate chips

¼ cup vegan cocoa powder

⅛ teaspoon salt

3 tablespoons vegan margarine, divided

2 ounces silken tofu, divided

¼ cup plus 1 tablespoon granulated sugar

1 teaspoon vanilla extract

½ cup chopped pecans

¼ cup plus 2 tablespoons all-purpose flour

2 teaspoons instant coffee granules

2 tablespoons coffee liqueur

1 cup water

VEGAN CHOCOLATE CHIPS
Some popular brands of chocolate chips are "accidentally vegan." Check the label of grocery store brands to find a vegan option or order them online.

1 Add the chocolate chips, cocoa, salt, and 2 tablespoons margarine to a small microwave-safe bowl. Microwave on high 1 minute; stir well. Microwave in additional 20-second increments if necessary until the margarine and chocolate are melted. Set aside to cool.

2 Add half of the tofu to a medium mixing bowl. Whisk or beat with a mixer until the tofu is smooth. Gradually add the ¼ cup sugar, continuing to whisk or beat; set aside.

3 Add the remaining tofu and vanilla to a mixing bowl; use a whisk or handheld mixer to beat. Stir in the cooled chocolate mixture, pecans, flour, instant coffee, and coffee liqueur and continue to mix until all ingredients are thoroughly combined.

4 Transfer a third of the beaten tofu to the chocolate mixture; stir to loosen the batter. Gently fold in the remaining tofu.

5 Treat the bottom and sides of a 1-quart metal pan with 2 teaspoons of the remaining margarine. Add 1 tablespoon sugar to the pan; shake and roll to coat the pan with the sugar. Dump out and discard any extra sugar. Transfer the chocolate batter to the pan.

continued on next page

Molten Fudge Pudding Cake—*continued*

6 Treat one side of a 15" piece of aluminum foil with the remaining teaspoon of margarine. Place the foil greased-side down over the top of the pan; crimp around the edges of the pan to form a seal.

7 Pour the water into the Instant Pot®. Place the trivet in the pot and set the cake on the trivet.

8 Lock the lid into place, press the Manual button, and adjust timer to 20 minutes.

9 When the timer beeps, quick-release pressure until float valve drops and then unlock lid. Transfer the cake to a wire rack. Remove foil cover.

10 Let rest 10–15 minutes. To serve, either spoon from the pan or run a knife around the edge of the pan, place a serving plate over the metal pan, and invert to transfer the cake.

Maple-Glazed Sweet Potatoes

You can remove the sugar from this recipe, if you like, by replacing it with a sweetener such as stevia. Maple-Glazed Sweet Potatoes are a great side dish for any autumn feast. If you're thinking of doubling the recipe, you may want to prepare it as is, in two batches.

- **Hands-On Time: 10 minutes**
- **Cook Time: 25 minutes**

Serves 2

1 cup water

4 cups peeled and diced sweet potatoes

1 tablespoon vegan margarine

¼ cup maple syrup

1 tablespoon light brown sugar

⅓ cup chopped pecans

1 Preheat the oven to 375°F.

2 Pour the water into the Instant Pot® and add the potatoes. Lock the lid into place. Press the Manual button and adjust timer to 5 minutes. When the timer beeps, let pressure release naturally for 10 minutes. Quick-release any remaining pressure until float valve drops and then unlock lid.

3 Drain the sweet potatoes in a colander. Place the margarine, syrup, and sugar in a small bowl and microwave about 30 seconds, or until the margarine is melted.

4 In a medium mixing bowl, toss the sweet potatoes, margarine mixture, and pecans, then pour into the casserole dish. Bake 10 minutes.

Glazed Lemon Poppy Seed Cake

As if poppy seed muffins weren't delicious enough, this recipe builds the treat into a whole cake, and then pours a delicious glaze over it. Make this cake ahead of time if you can; the flavor improves if you seal it in plastic wrap and store it for a day or two before you serve it.

- **Hands-On Time: 10 minutes**
- **Cook Time: 20 minutes**

Serves 8

½ cup vegan margarine
1 cup granulated sugar
2 ounces silken tofu
1 teaspoon vanilla extract
2 medium lemons
1¼ cups all-purpose flour
1 teaspoon baking soda
1 teaspoon baking powder
¼ teaspoon salt
⅔ cup unsweetened soy milk
⅓ cup poppy seeds
2 cups water
½ cup powdered sugar, sifted

1 Add the margarine and sugar to a medium mixing bowl; beat until light and fluffy. Beat in the tofu, vanilla, grated zest from 1 lemon, and juice from 1 lemon.

2 Mix together the flour, baking soda, baking powder, and salt in a separate medium bowl. Add the flour mixture and milk in three batches to the margarine mixture, mixing after each addition. Stir in the poppy seeds.

3 Treat a 4-cup soufflé dish or Bundt pan with nonstick spray. Transfer the batter to the pan.

4 Treat a 15" square of heavy-duty aluminum foil with nonstick spray. Place the foil, treated side down, over the pan; crimp around the edges to seal.

5 Pour the water into the Instant Pot® and insert the trivet. Place the pan on the rack over the foil strips. Lock the lid into place, press the Manual button, and adjust timer to 20 minutes.

6 When the timer beeps, let pressure release naturally until float valve drops and then unlock lid. Remove the lid. Transfer the cake to a cooling rack. Remove foil cover.

7 To make the glaze, whisk the juice and grated zest from the remaining lemon together with the powdered sugar. Transfer the cake to a serving platter and drizzle the glaze over the top.

US/Metric Conversion Chart

VOLUME CONVERSIONS

US Volume Measure	Metric Equivalent
⅛ teaspoon	0.5 milliliter
¼ teaspoon	1 milliliter
½ teaspoon	2 milliliters
1 teaspoon	5 milliliters
½ tablespoon	7 milliliters
1 tablespoon (3 teaspoons)	15 milliliters
2 tablespoons (1 fluid ounce)	30 milliliters
¼ cup (4 tablespoons)	60 milliliters
⅓ cup	90 milliliters
½ cup (4 fluid ounces)	125 milliliters
⅔ cup	160 milliliters
¾ cup (6 fluid ounces)	180 milliliters
1 cup (16 tablespoons)	250 milliliters
1 pint (2 cups)	500 milliliters
1 quart (4 cups)	1 liter (about)

WEIGHT CONVERSIONS

US Weight Measure	Metric Equivalent
½ ounce	15 grams
1 ounce	30 grams
2 ounces	60 grams
3 ounces	85 grams
¼ pound (4 ounces)	115 grams
½ pound (8 ounces)	225 grams
¾ pound (12 ounces)	340 grams
1 pound (16 ounces)	454 grams

OVEN TEMPERATURE CONVERSIONS

Degrees Fahrenheit	Degrees Celsius
200 degrees F	95 degrees C
250 degrees F	120 degrees C
275 degrees F	135 degrees C
300 degrees F	150 degrees C
325 degrees F	160 degrees C
350 degrees F	180 degrees C
375 degrees F	190 degrees C
400 degrees F	205 degrees C
425 degrees F	220 degrees C
450 degrees F	230 degrees C

BAKING PAN SIZES

American	Metric
8 x 1½ inch round baking pan	20 x 4 cm cake tin
9 x 1½ inch round baking pan	23 x 3.5 cm cake tin
11 x 7 x 1½ inch baking pan	28 x 18 x 4 cm baking tin
13 x 9 x 2 inch baking pan	30 x 20 x 5 cm baking tin
2 quart rectangular baking dish	30 x 20 x 3 cm baking tin
15 x 10 x 2 inch baking pan	30 x 25 x 2 cm baking tin (Swiss roll tin)
9 inch pie plate	22 x 4 or 23 x 4 cm pie plate
7 or 8 inch springform pan	18 or 20 cm springform or loose bottom cake tin
9 x 5 x 3 inch loaf pan	23 x 13 x 7 cm or 2 lb narrow loaf or pâté tin
1½ quart casserole	1.5 liter casserole
2 quart casserole	2 liter casserole

Index

Note: Page numbers in **bold** indicate recipe category lists.

About the Author

Britt Brandon is a certified personal trainer and certified fitness nutrition specialist (certified by the International Sports Sciences Association, ISSA) who has enjoyed writing books that focus on clean eating, fitness, and unique health, promoting ingredients such as apple cider vinegar, coconut oil, and aloe vera for Adams Media. In her time with Adams, she has published eleven books, including *The Everything® Green Smoothies Book*, *The Everything® Eating Clean Cookbook*, *What Color Is Your Smoothie?*, *The Everything® Eating Clean Cookbook for Vegetarians*, *The Everything® Healthy Green Drinks Book*, and *The Everything® Guide to Pregnancy Nutrition & Health*. As a competitive athlete, trainer, mom of three children, and fitness and nutrition blogger on her own website (UltimateFitMom.com), she is well versed in the holistic approaches to keeping oneself in top performing condition.